THE
TOP 100
LOW-SALT
RECIPES

THE
TOP 100
LOW-SALT
RECIPES

Christine Bailey

CONTROL YOUR BLOOD PRESSURE
REDUCE YOUR RISK OF HEART DISEASE AND STROKE

DUNCAN BAIRD PUBLISHERS

LONDON

The Top 100 Low-Salt Recipes
Christine Bailey

First published in the United Kingdom and Ireland in 2009 by
Duncan Baird Publishers Ltd
Sixth Floor
Castle House
75–76 Wells Street
London W1T 3QH

Conceived, created and designed by
Duncan Baird Publishers

Managing Editor: Grace Cheetham
Editor: Nicole Bator
Managing Designer: Daniel Sturges
Designer: Sue Bush
Commissioned photography: Simon Scott
Food stylist: Mari Mererid Williams
Prop stylist: Helen Trent

British Library Cataloguing-in-Publication Data:
A CIP record for this book is available from the British Library

ISBN: 978-1-84483-756-4

10 9 8 7 6 5 4 3 2 1

Typeset in Helvetica Condensed
Colour reproduction by Colourscan, Singapore
Printed in China by Imago

I would like to thank everyone at Duncan
Baird Publishers, especially Grace, for their
ongoing help and advice with this book during
its production. My thanks also to my wonderful husband Chris and our children Nathan,
Isaac and Simeon for their endless support,
encouragement and tireless taste-testing of
all the recipes.

Publisher's Note
The information in this book is not intended as a substitute for
professional medical advice and treatment. If you are pregnant
or breastfeeding or have any special dietary requirements or
medical conditions, it is recommended that you consult a
medical professional before following any of the information
or recipes contained in this book. Duncan Baird Publishers,
or any other persons who have been involved in working on
this publication, cannot accept responsibility for any errors
or omissions, inadvertent or not, that may be found in the
recipes or text, or for any problems that may arise as a result
of preparing one of these recipes or following the advice
contained in this work.

Notes on the Recipes
Unless otherwise stated:
Use medium eggs, fruit and vegetables
Use unsalted butter and fresh ingredients, including herbs
Do not mix metric and imperial measurements
1 tsp = 5ml   1 tbsp = 15ml   1 cup = 250ml

Symbols are used to identify even small amounts of an
ingredient, such as the seeds symbol for sunflower oil.
Dairy foods in this book may include cow's, goat's or sheep's
milk. The vegetarian symbol is given to recipes using cheese;
please check the manufacturer's labelling before purchase to
ensure cheeses are vegetarian. Ensure that only the relevantly
identified foods are given to anyone with a food allergy or
intolerance.

contents

KEY TO SYMBOLS

Ⓥ Suitable for vegetarians: These dishes contain no meat, fish or poultry. Often high in potassium, they can improve mineral balance and lower blood pressure. Check labels to ensure that cheeses are suitable for vegetarians.

Contains dairy: Dairy allergies can cause asthma-like symptoms, abdominal pains and eczema. Try low-salt alternatives, such as fortified soya, rice, oat or nut milk, yogurts and cheeses. Use coconut or olive oil instead of butter.

Contains eggs: Try using 25–50g/1–2oz tofu mashed with a little water or 1 tbsp arrowroot mixed with 3 tbsp water for each egg, or a commercial egg replacer.

Contains gluten: Intolerance to gluten, a protein in wheat, rye, barley and oats, can cause inflammation, digestive problems and other ailments. Gluten-free grains include buckwheat, millet, rice, quinoa and corn.

Contains nuts: Substitute different unsalted seeds for nuts if necessary.

Contains seeds: If necessary, omit seeds or use dried fruit or oats in baking instead. Replace seed oils with olive oil.

Contains sugar: Agave, fructose and xylitol sweeten without raising blood sugar levels in the same way as regular sugar.

Contains wheat: Alternatives include corn, buckwheat, rice, quinoa, barley, rye and millet. Gluten-free flour mixes and wheat-free breads are available – check salt levels as they can vary between brands.

INTRODUCTION

Enjoying great, healthy, home-cooked food with family and friends is one of life's greatest pleasures. But in our fast-paced world, it may seem easier to microwave a ready meal or phone for a takeaway than cook a wholesome meal from scratch. With so many processed and time-saving food products available, it is tempting to throw a jar, packet or can in the supermarket trolley instead of heading to the fresh produce aisle. And all too often in this fast-food world, our diets fall short. Rather than nourishing our bodies, the foods we eat are actually damaging our health. This is particularly true when it comes to the amount of sodium we consume from salt in our diets. We are becoming increasingly aware of the need to watch our salt intake – and for good reason. Eating too much salt can raise blood pressure, increase the risk of heart disease and stroke and lead to other health problems, such as certain cancers, kidney disease and osteoporosis. Yet most of us eat far too much salt. It is estimated that, on average, adults consume up to 12g salt a day, more than twice the World Health Organization's daily maximum recommended intake of 5g a day – about one teaspoon of salt.

For many people, reducing their salt intake equates to bland food or spending hours in the kitchen preparing complicated meals. But with a little savvy shopping and the help of the 100 recipes in this book, you will discover how flavourful low-salt cooking can be.

ABOUT THIS BOOK

This book aims to inspire you to cook recipes that are low in salt and full of nutritious ingredients. It will show you how to use flavourings, herbs and spices as alternatives to salt to create healthy, tantalizing meals you can enjoy every day. Whether cooking for one, feeding a family or entertaining friends on a special occasion, you will find an irresistible selection of ideas for delicious breakfasts, lunches, side dishes, teas, snacks, dinners and desserts. Many of the recipes are quick and easy to prepare, while others can be assembled in advance to take the hassle out of mealtimes.

All the recipes have been created to make the most of the flavours that wholesome, fresh, good-quality ingredients offer – so there's no compromising on taste. You will find inspiration from around the world to give bold, fresh flavours to your food: lemongrass, lime and ginger from Asia; pomegranate molasses from the Middle East; and fiery chillies, paprika and peppers from South America.

Many people follow a low-salt diet in order to keep their blood pressure down or to improve their overall health and energy levels. These recipes, therefore, are based around superfoods, such as fresh fruits and vegetables, heart-healthy oils and lean fish and meat, to provide plenty of essential nutrients while also being low in saturated fats and sugars.

These recipes contain no added salt. Occasionally, ingredients are used that have some added salt, such as bread, but each recipe contains less than 0.35g salt (0.14g sodium) per serving. Read food labels carefully to find the best low-salt versions of ingredients that do contain salt.

WHAT IS SALT?

Salt is the common name for sodium chloride and it is the sodium that is most damaging to health. Sodium is needed by the body in small amounts to help maintain the right balance of fluids, to assist in transmitting nerve impulses and to aid the contraction and relaxation of muscles. The kidneys help regulate sodium levels in the body – when levels are high, excess sodium is excreted in the urine. When sodium intake becomes too high, the kidneys aren't able to eliminate all of the excess and it starts to accumulate in the blood. This leads to excess fluid retention and increased blood pressure and can result in a number of health problems.

SALT AND HEALTH

There is now strong evidence to suggest that a high intake of salt can lead to high blood pressure and damage your heart. Salt makes our bodies retain water, and if we eat too much salt, then our bodies hold on to too much water. The extra fluid retained by the body leads to an increase in the pressure in our blood – resulting in high blood pressure (hypertension).

This can cause long-term health problems – in fact people with high blood pressure are three times more likely to develop heart disease and strokes. High blood pressure accounts for 60 per cent of all strokes and 50 per cent of all heart disease. It is estimated that reducing salt intake by 6g a day, coupled with a healthier lifestyle, could reduce the risk of heart attacks worldwide by 18 per cent and strokes by 24 per cent. This equates to preventing approximately 2.6 million deaths each year. A high intake of salt can also lead to other health problems, including an increased risk of certain cancers, kidney disease, obesity, fluid retention and asthma attacks. It can also lead to an increase in the amount of calcium excreted in the urine, which may contribute to osteoporosis and significantly raise the risk of fractures.

And it's not just adults who are affected. Children are also consuming far too much salt, which may increase their risk of developing diseases later in life. Dietary surveys estimate that boys aged four to six are consuming 5.2g salt per day – over 70 per cent more than the recommended maximum intake. Meanwhile, girls in the same age group are consuming 4.6g per day – more than 50 per cent above the recommended maximum. Tempting and convenient as they are, the abundance of ready meals, pre-packed processed foods and snack foods, such as crisps, biscuits, sweets and fizzy drinks, all contribute significantly to this high-salt diet.

Don't be fooled into thinking that other forms of salt are any healthier – rock salt and sea salt are no different from ordinary table salt. Flavoured salts such as garlic, onion and celery salts should also be avoided. Several reduced-sodium salts are now widely available; these taste a little different from traditional sea salt and contain a high percentage of potassium. If you have heart or kidney problems, you should consult your doctor before using these products because of their potassium chloride levels.

Many people mistakenly believe that we need more salt during hot weather or strenuous exercise as it is lost through increased perspiration. In fact, it is water that needs to be replaced. The body is able to make adjustments and can easily survive on just 1g salt per day. Muscle cramps are normally a sign of dehydration rather than a lack of salt, so remember to drink plenty of water especially on hot days or before, during and after exercise.

MAIN SOURCES OF SALT

Fast food, takeaways, restaurant meals and canteen meals can be very high in salt, but 80 per cent of the salt in our diets comes from processed and packaged foods that

HIGH-SALT FOODS

The following foods are often high in salt/sodium. Check food labels because brands can vary. Look out for low-salt versions of your favourites.

Bakery and Grains

Breads, especially flavoured breads, pittas, bagels, crumpets, brioche; breadcrumbs

Breakfast cereals

Biscuits, sweet and savoury

Pastries, such as croissants, Danish pastries, apple turnovers

Commercial desserts and cakes, cheesecakes, pies, fruit tarts, muffins

Batter, coating, pancake and cake mixes

Dairy

Hard and semi-hard cheeses such as Cheddar, Cheshire, Parmesan, pecorino, Gouda, Edam, havarti, Jarlsberg, halloumi, feta and smoked cheeses

Soft cheeses, such as cottage cheese (especially flavoured varieties), and cheese spreads

Salted butters and spreads

Canned Foods

Beans and lentils in salted water

Baked beans

Olives and capers

Fish or vegetables in brine

Soups

Cooking sauces

Canned spaghetti

Meat, Fish and Seafood

Sausages, sausage rolls

Salami, smoked meats, bacon, corned beef

Ham, especially Parma ham

Smoked fish, such as mackerel fillets, smoked salmon and trout

Ready-made fish dishes, such as fish pies, fish cakes and fish fingers

Fish pastes and pâtés; spreads, such as taramasalata; anchovies

Condiments

Soy sauce, teriyaki sauce, barbecue sauce, miso, ketchup, tomato purée, mustard, mayonnaise, pickles, salad dressings

Gravy granules, stock cubes and powders, yeast extracts

Seasoned salts, such as celery, onion and garlic salt

Snack Foods and Beverages

Crisps, cheesy biscuits and salted crackers, pretzels, salted nuts

Shop-bought sandwiches, chips, burgers, pies, pizza, ready-made quiches and flans

Ready meals, such as pasta dishes; Chinese and Indian meals

Hot chocolate drinks; tomato and vegetable juices; many fizzy drinks

we use at home. Staples such as breads, cheese and breakfast cereals as well as cooking sauces, soups, condiments like tomato ketchup and mayonnaise, and even bought puddings, cakes and biscuits, can contribute a lot to our daily salt intake – especially if eaten on a daily basis. A typical teriyaki marinade can have up to 2g salt per tablespoon (one third of the daily maximum recommended adult intake) and Dijon mustard can have 1g per tablespoon.

SWITCHING TO A LOW-SALT DIET

Changing to a low-salt diet doesn't have to mean your food will taste bland. In fact, too much salt can actually mask the flavour of food. As you start to reduce the amount of salt you use, you will begin to discover a whole new range of exciting flavours. It will also force you to cook more foods from scratch and focus on good-quality, fresh ingredients for flavour – which will also benefit your overall health. Adjust

SALT LEVELS – HIGH or LOW?

Choose foods that have a low sodium or salt content per 100g. The table below shows the levels of sodium and salt to look for per 100g of food. Remember to consider portion sizes. Yeast extracts, for example, are high in sodium but an average serving is only about 4g, which contains 0.2g sodium (0.5g salt).

Salt content	Amount of sodium in grams per 100g	Amount of salt in grams per 100g
HIGH	more than 0.5g	more than 1.25g
MEDIUM	0.1–0.5g	0.25g–1.25g
LOW	less than 0.1g	less than 0.25g

your salt intake gradually: it normally takes three to four weeks for your taste buds to adapt to less salt.

READING FOOD LABELS

Food labels can be something of a mine-field, especially when it comes to working out how much salt a product contains. Processed foods list the main ingredients in order of weight. Although salt is very light in weight and may therefore appear towards the end of an ingredients list, that product may still contain a hefty amount of salt, so be sure to always check the nutritional information too.

Food labels often list the sodium content of the product rather than the salt (sodium chloride) content. This can be confusing if you're trying to keep track of how much salt you're eating. One gram of sodium is equivalent to 2.5g salt, so to convert sodium to salt you need to multiply the sodium figure by 2.5. For example, crisps contain on average 0.57g sodium per 100g, which is equivalent to 1.43g salt.

Look out for ingredients that contain the word sodium, which means the food probably has a high sodium content. These ingredients can occur in a wide range of foods and include additives such as monosodium glutamate (a flavour enhancer), sodium nitrate (a preservative), sodium bicarbonate (a raising agent) and sodium saccharin (a sweetener).

COOKING TECHNIQUES

Experiment with different cooking methods to help retain the natural flavours in the food. Stir-frying is a quick and simple way to cook vegetables, meat and fish. Adding spices and herbs, fruit, wine, seasoned vinegars and flavoured oils can transform a familiar dish into a taste sensation. If you like soy sauce, try tamari instead – a wheat-free version that is often lower in salt than regular brands.

Pan-frying meat or fish before adding it to a dish and roasting, barbecuing and grilling are all great ways to concentrate flavours and let the natural sugars in the food caramelize – creating a sweeter, richer taste. Use salt-free marinades and spice rubs – they not only add flavour, they keep the food moist while it cooks.

Steaming, another healthy and quick cooking method, prevents vegetables from becoming too soggy and leaching out valuable nutrients and flavour. Fish is wonderful steamed – wrap it in lettuce leaves, vine leaves or greaseproof paper to retain the juices. You can also tuck in a few slices of lemon or lime, fresh herbs or more exotic spices to create exciting flavours.

TOP TIPS FOR REDUCING SALT INTAKE

- Ditch the salt shaker. Keep it off the table and don't add salt before tasting food.
- Use fresh or frozen vegetables and fresh poultry, fish and lean meat.
- Use less salt in cooking. You can reduce or even eliminate the salt from most recipes without affecting flavour.
- Avoid 'instant' and 'flavoured' packaged and processed foods.
- Choose canned foods packed in water only. Avoid foods canned in brine or labelled as cured, smoked or pickled.
- Make your own healthy snacks, such as cinnamon-flavoured popcorn, or snack on unsalted nuts and seeds.
- Replace high-salt breakfast cereals with porridge and home-made muesli and granola (see pages 27–9).
- Make your own stock (see page 18) or reserve the water when steaming vegetables to use as a flavoursome broth.
- Use olive oil, unsalted butter or unsalted nut and seed butters for spreading.
- Make your own marinades, chilli pastes, spice blends and salad dressings.
- Use wine and fruit juices to add moisture and flavour.

- Eat more fruit and vegetables – rich in potassium, they can help balance the sodium levels in the body.
- Flavour your food with fresh and dried herbs and spices.
- Read food labels, especially on staples like bread and cereals; salt levels vary among brands, so choose wisely.

HOW POTASSIUM CAN HELP

Reducing your sodium intake is only half the battle. Sodium is just one of several important mineral salts present in the body – others include potassium and magnesium. For optimum health, these minerals need to be in proper balance. Potassium and sodium are intricately related in the body and work together to maintain the correct water balance and proper nerve and muscle impulses. The more sodium you eat, the more potassium you need to keep the balance in check. Too much sodium coupled with too little potassium can lead to cardiovascular disease, cancers and water retention. The best sources of potassium are fruit and vegetables (see list below).

TOP POTASSIUM-RICH FOODS

Most fruit and vegetables are rich in potassium, so aim to eat at least five, but ideally seven, portions a day. Here are some great choices:

- Asparagus
- Avocado
- Banana
- Celery
- Cucumber
- Dark green leafy vegetables, such as spinach, broccoli, Brussels sprouts, kale, Swiss chard
- Fennel
- Fresh or dried figs and apricots; prunes
- Honeydew melon
- Papaya
- Potato

SMART SHOPPING

If preparing flavourful meals without the salt shaker sounds like a tall order, then forward planning and organization make it much easier. The first step is keeping a well-stocked kitchen. The following lists provide a useful starting point. There are lots of really good low-sodium ingredients here, as well as many healthy foods, herbs and flavourings that are frequently used in the recipes in this book. Most of them can be found in good supermarkets. If you can't find them, try your local health food store.

Foods for Your Fridge

- Cheese: low-salt varieties – check labels, but good options include goats' cheese, mozzarella, ricotta, Gruyère, Emmental, cream cheese
- Eggs: preferably organic and enriched with omega-3
- Fresh fish, poultry and lean meat
- Fresh fruit and vegetables
- Fresh herbs
- Fruit juices, such as orange and grape, for flavouring
- Milk: semi-skimmed or skimmed; or dairy-free alternatives, such as soya, nut, oat or quinoa milk
- Nuts and seeds: unsalted; store in the fridge for freshness
- Nut and seed butters: unsalted; rich in healthy omega-3 and omega-6 fats
- Tofu (soya bean curd): plain firm or silken – avoid smoked versions
- Yogurt: live natural yogurt, sheeps' or goats' milk yogurt, soya yogurt

Storecupboard Staples

- Brown basmati rice, wholemeal pasta, egg noodles, buckwheat or soba noodles
- Canned coconut milk
- Canned fish in water or olive oil
- Dried herbs and spices
- Good-quality dark chocolate
- Harissa paste, low-salt tomato purée
- Honey, fructose, xylitol and agave nectar
- Low-salt breads, pitta breads, crackers and tortillas (look for less than 1.1g salt per 100g); plain muffins and tea cakes
- Marinated artichoke hearts in oil or water
- Mirin, tamari (wheat-free soy sauce), reduced-salt soy sauce
- Oats, oatmeal, low-salt oat cakes, rye and barley flakes, wheat bran
- Olive oil or coconut oil (for cooking); hempseed, flaxseed or extra virgin olive oil (for dressings)
- Quinoa, millet, barley, buckwheat
- Roasted red peppers in oil
- Tahini (sesame seed paste)
- Vanilla extract, rosewater
- Wholemeal flour, buckwheat flour, rice flour, gluten-free flour mixes
- Wine and spirits (for cooking)

THE RECIPES IN THIS BOOK

Olive oil is used for cooking in these recipes. A monounsaturated fat, it is less susceptible to damage from heat, which can transform oils into harmful trans fats. Another excellent cooking oil is coconut oil, which does not raise cholesterol or produce harmful trans fats when cooked.

Some recipes call for a little sugar or honey to sweeten them. Fructose is a natural sugar alternative that does not raise blood sugar levels in the same way as regular sugar does. It is also lower in calories. Xylitol and agave nectar are also excellent natural substitutes for regular sugar and they do not have such a negative effect on blood sugar levels. These are readily available in health food shops and most supermarkets.

Whenever possible, choose fresh, seasonal food and opt to buy as much organic produce as your budget will allow – especially meat and dairy produce.

Eating seasonally will ensure the food is fresher, packed with vital nutrients and full of natural flavour – all of which will make it easier for you and the people you cook for to ditch the salt.

SPECIAL DIETS

Each recipe comes with an explanation of its health benefits as well as some serving suggestions to enable you to create a nutritionally balanced meal or snack. They have been created to appeal to the whole family, making meal-planning easier and quicker. Many of the recipes are also suitable for particular diets. Whether you are a vegetarian or have an allergy or sensitivity to gluten, wheat, dairy produce, eggs, nuts, seeds or sugar, you will find a range of healthy and delicious recipes to suit your every need – without worrying about unwanted reactions. Check the easy-to-read symbols at the top of each recipe for immediate reference.

GETTING AHEAD

For delicious low-salt meals in minutes, it's worth preparing a few simple basics in advance. These versatile staples can be made ahead of time; the stock, peppers and tomato sauce can also be frozen.

Asian-style Vinaigrette

This aromatic dressing is delicious on salads or served with meat and fish.

Makes 135ml/4½fl oz/generous ½ cup
Preparation: 10 minutes

1 garlic clove, chopped
1 red chilli, deseeded and chopped
1 lemongrass stalk, thinly sliced
1 tsp chopped root ginger
2 tbsp Thai fish sauce
2 tbsp honey
4 tbsp lime juice
freshly ground black pepper

1 Put all the ingredients in a blender, season with pepper and blend briefly until smooth.

Home-made Vegetable Stock

Vary the vegetables in this recipe according to what you have available and what's in season. Save the water used when steaming vegetables – it makes a great basic stock.

Makes 1 litre/35fl oz/4 cups
Preparation + Cooking: 10 + 45 minutes

1 onion, sliced
2 carrots, peeled and sliced
2 leeks, sliced
2 celery sticks with leaves, chopped
2 bay leaves
1 handful parsley sprigs
1 handful broccoli stems

1 Put all the ingredients in a large saucepan and cover with boiling water. Bring to the boil, then reduce the heat and simmer for 30–45 minutes until tender.

2 Strain the stock through a sieve and discard the vegetables. Leave to cool. Cover and chill in the fridge.

Roasted Peppers

Sweet and full of flavour, roasted peppers are delicious and so simple to prepare. They are divine in salads and wraps, stirred into couscous or added to pasta. For variety and to add colour, you can prepare green, yellow and orange peppers in the same way.

Serves: 4
Preparation + Cooking: 5 + 15 minutes

4 red peppers, halved and deseeded

1 Preheat the grill to high. Put the peppers, cut-side down, on a baking sheet. Grill for 15 minutes, or until the skins blacken.
2 Transfer the peppers to a bowl, cover with cling film and leave to cool.
3 Peel off and discard the skins.

Tomato Sauce

This tangy sauce makes a great base for soups, stews and pasta sauces.

Serves: 4–6
Preparation + Cooking: 10 + 30 minutes

1 tbsp olive oil
1 onion
2 garlic cloves
2 carrots, peeled and cut into chunks
1 butternut squash, peeled, deseeded and cut into chunks
400g/14oz canned plum tomatoes, no added salt
300g/10½oz tomatoes, chopped
300ml/10½fl oz/1¼ cups Home-made Vegetable Stock (see page 18)
2 tbsp chopped parsley

1 Heat the oil in a large saucepan, add the onion and garlic and cook over a medium heat for 3–4 minutes until soft. Add the remaining ingredients. Bring to the boil, reduce the heat and simmer for 20 minutes until the vegetables are tender.
2 Using a hand-held electric blender, blend the mixture for 2–3 minutes until smooth.

BREAKFASTS

Some of the worst-offending high-salt foods include breakfast cereals, breads and morning pastries – staples in many homes and especially popular with children. In this chapter, you'll find a mouthwatering selection of healthy home-made alternatives, such as moreish Vanilla & Spice Granola, delicious Blueberry Buttermilk Pancakes and savoury Oat Muffins with Eggs & Spinach. Discover how to use flavourful ingredients like tangy fruits and fruit juices, crunchy nuts and seeds, and a variety of fresh and dried herbs and spices to create amazing flavours without adding salt. Loaded with nutrients, these recipes will also give you a great start to the day – and keep you alert and focused, without those mid-morning energy slumps.

Ⓥ Ⓕ Ⓥ ▶ ⊛

mango & oat smoothie

SERVES 4

PREPARATION + COOKING
10 + 4 minutes

STORAGE
Store the oat topping in an
airtight container for 3–4 weeks.
The smoothie is best drunk
immediately, but it will keep in
the fridge for 4–5 hours.

SERVE THIS WITH…
Baked Eggs with Harissa
(see page 38)

HEALTH BENEFITS
Bananas are rich in potassium,
an important mineral for
promoting healthy blood
pressure. They also contain
pectin, a fibre that helps relieve
ulcers and inflammation
in the digestive tract and
lowers cholesterol.

Smoothies are a great way to start the day.
Simple to prepare, they can be whizzed up
in minutes using nutritious, flavoursome
ingredients. The oat and nut topping on this
smoothie will keep you energized all morning.

1 tbsp olive oil
100g/3½oz/1 cup rolled oats
55g/2oz/½ cup hazelnuts,
    chopped
55g/2oz/½ cup flaked almonds
1 tbsp ground flaxseed

1 mango, peeled, stoned and
    chopped
2 bananas, chopped
150ml/5fl oz/⅔ cup natural
    yogurt
juice of ½ orange

1 Heat the oil in a non-stick frying pan, add the oats and
toast, stirring occasionally, for 2–3 minutes until golden.
Add the hazelnuts and almonds and toast for a further
1 minute. Remove from the heat and leave to cool, then
stir in the flaxseed.
2 Put the mango, bananas, yogurt and orange juice in a
blender or food processor. Blend until smooth. Pour into
glasses and top with the oats. Serve with a spoon.

pineapple, lime & avocado smoothie

This creamy smoothie is packed with heart protecting nutrients. Avocados are rich in healthy monounsaturated fat, fibre, folic acid, iron and vitamin E. They are also one of the top fruit sources of potassium, which is essential for healthy blood pressure and reducing fluid retention.

1 avocado, halved and stoned	1 tsp lime juice
500ml/17fl oz/2 cups fresh pineapple juice	2 tsp honey

1 Remove the flesh from the avocado and place in a blender or food processor. Add the remaining ingredients and blend for 1–2 minutes until smooth and creamy.
2 Pour into glasses and serve immediately.

SERVES 2

PREPARATION TIME
5 minutes

STORAGE
Best drunk immediately.

SERVE THIS WITH...
Vanilla & Spice Granola
(see page 27)

HEALTH BENEFITS
Pineapple contains bromelain, an enzyme that aids digestion by helping to break down proteins. It possesses anti-inflammatory properties and can help reduce the stickiness of blood, making it useful for conditions such as angina and thrombosis. It is a useful diuretic too and can help balance body fluids.

003

Ⓥ

spicy tomato juice

SERVES 4

PREPARATION
10 minutes

STORAGE
Best drunk immediately but
will keep in the fridge for up
to 12 hours.

SERVE THIS WITH...
Oat Muffins with Eggs & Spinach
(see page 34)

HEALTH BENEFITS
Celery contains active
compounds called pthalides,
which relax the muscles of the
arteries that regulate blood
pressure. Both cucumber and
celery are powerful diuretics
and, being rich in potassium,
are useful for relieving water
retention and combating excess
sodium intake.

Many shop-bought drinks, including tomato
juice, contain surprisingly high levels of
salt and other additives. Making your own
will ensure they include nothing but fresh,
nutritious ingredients. This juice has plenty
of vitamin C and beta-carotene to help
support the immune system.

10 large ripe tomatoes, cut into
   chunks
1 red pepper, deseeded and cut
   into chunks
3 celery sticks, roughly
   chopped

½ large cucumber, cut into
   sticks
2.5cm/1in piece root ginger,
   peeled
crushed ice, to serve (optional)

1 Push all the ingredients through a juicer.
2 Serve in glasses over ice, if you like.

cranberry & cherry compote

This delicious, salt-free compote is packed full of heart-protecting and immune-boosting antioxidants. Spoon it over pancakes or muesli or stir it into natural yogurt for a sweet treat.

115g/4oz/1 cup dried
   cranberries
115g/4oz/1 cup dried cherries
55g/2oz/¾ cup dried apricots
2 apples, peeled, cored and
   chopped

4 tbsp apple juice
1 cinnamon stick
5 cloves
2 tbsp grated orange zest

1 Put the dried fruit in a bowl and cover with warm water. Leave to soak for 15 minutes, then drain.
2 Put the soaked fruit in a saucepan with the remaining ingredients. Bring to the boil, then reduce the heat and simmer for 10–15 minutes, breaking up the fruit until the mixture thickens. Serve hot or at room temperature.

SERVES 4

PREPARATION + COOKING
5 + 15 minutes + soaking

STORAGE
Make in advance and keep in the fridge for up to 5 days or freeze for up to 1 month.

SERVE THIS WITH...
Lemon Buckwheat Blinis
   (see page 32)

HEALTH BENEFITS
Cranberries and cherries are rich in antioxidants, particularly vitamin C and flavonoids called anthocyanins, which support the body's immune system and protect against cancer and heart disease. They also work together to strengthen the veins and arteries, aiding circulation.

005

cardamom & fruit compote

This aromatic concoction is great on its own for breakfast or as a healthy dessert. Dried fruit is an excellent way to add flavour without adding salt. High in soluble fibre, it also boosts energy and can help lower cholesterol.

SERVES 4–6

PREPARATION + COOKING
5 + 15 minutes

STORAGE
Make in advance and keep in the fridge for up to 1 week.

SERVE THIS WITH...
Apricot & Almond Muesli
(see page 28)

HEALTH BENEFITS
Prunes are particularly high in antioxidants, which can help protect the body against cancers, heart disease and ageing. They also supply plenty of potassium, useful for lowering high blood pressure and eliminating excess sodium from the body.

100g/3½oz/½ cup dried apricots
140g/5oz/1½ cups dried pears
   or peaches, chopped
100g/3½oz/½ cup prunes,
   pitted
90g/3¼oz/½ cup dried cherries
100g/3½oz/½ cup dried figs
1 tbsp cardamom seeds,
   crushed
4 cloves
juice of 3 oranges
1 tbsp orange flower water

1 Put all the ingredients in a heavy-based saucepan. Add 250ml/9floz/1 cup water, bring to the boil, then reduce the heat and simmer for 15 minutes or until the fruit is tender.
2 Serve warm or at room temperature.

Ⓥ Ⓖ Ⓕ Ⓒ Ⓨ

vanilla & spice granola

This delicious version of the breakfast favourite is full of nutritious, slow energy-releasing grains plus antioxidant-rich berries. The nuts and seeds supply the body with plenty of protein and essential fats to keep you energized and focused until lunchtime.

200g/7oz/2 cups rolled oats	5 tbsp apple juice
115g/4oz/1¼ cups barley flakes	5 tbsp honey
55g/2oz/½ cup flaked almonds	3 tbsp olive oil
55g/2oz/½ cup chopped walnuts	2 tbsp vanilla extract
30g/1oz/¼ cup pumpkin seeds	1 tsp ground cinnamon
30g/1oz/¼ cup sunflower seeds	½ tsp ground nutmeg
3 tbsp sesame seeds	115g/4oz/¾ cup dried berries

1 Preheat the oven to 180°C/350°F/Gas 4. Put the oats, barley flakes, almonds, walnuts and seeds in a large bowl and mix well. In a separate bowl, mix together the apple juice, honey, oil, vanilla extract, cinnamon and nutmeg. Pour this mixture over the dry ingredients and stir well.
2 Tip the mixture on to two baking sheets and spread out evenly. Bake for 20 minutes, stirring occasionally, until golden. Remove from the oven and leave to cool. Mix in the dried berries and serve.

SERVES 4–6

PREPARATION + COOKING
10 + 20 minutes

STORAGE
Make in advance and store in an airtight container for up to 1 month.

SERVE THIS WITH...
Cardamom & Fruit Compote (see page 26)
natural yogurt or milk

HEALTH BENEFITS
Although nuts are high in fat, it is predominantly healthy monounsaturated fat, which can protect against heart disease. Nuts are also rich in other heart-friendly nutrients, including vitamin E, folate, calcium, magnesium and zinc.

apricot & almond muesli

HEALTH BENEFITS
Oats and wheat germ are rich in slow-releasing carbohydrates to keep energy levels sustained right through the morning. They also contain a type of soluble fibre called beta-glucan, which is useful for balancing blood sugar levels and lowering cholesterol.

This nutrient-rich muesli is bursting with so much flavour, you won't miss the salt that is often added to shop-bought versions. Toasting the oats brings out their sweet nuttiness, and the dried apricots are a great source of iron.

olive oil, for greasing
250g/9oz/2½ cups rolled oats
30g/1oz/scant ¼ cup wheat
   germ
2 tbsp shredded unsweetened
   coconut flakes

1 tsp ground cinnamon
55g/2oz/½ cup chopped
   almonds
250ml/9floz/1 cup apple juice
55g/2oz/½ cup chopped dried
   apricots

SERVES 8

PREPARATION + COOKING
10 + 25 minutes

STORAGE
Make in advance and store in
an airtight container for up to
4 weeks.

SERVE THIS WITH...
Cardamom & Fruit Compote
   (see page 26)
fresh fruit
natural yogurt, milk, nut milk
   or coconut milk

1 Preheat the oven to 180°C/350°F/Gas 4. Lightly grease
three baking sheets with oil. Put the oats, wheat germ,
coconut, cinnamon, almonds and apple juice in a bowl
and mix well.

2 Spread the mixture out evenly on the baking sheets.
Bake for 25 minutes, stirring occasionally, until evenly
browned.

3 Remove from the oven and leave to cool. Stir in the
chopped apricots and serve.

> **Use millet
> or quinoa flakes to
> make this recipe
> suitable for anyone
> with a sensitivity to
> gluten.**

800

V

SERVES 4

PREPARATION + COOKING
5 + 10 minutes

STORAGE
Soak the oats in the fridge
overnight to speed up cooking
the following morning.

SERVE THIS WITH...
Pineapple, Lime & Avocado
  Smoothie (see page 23)
natural yogurt and toasted seeds
fresh or poached fruit

HEALTH BENEFITS
Cinnamon is a great natural
sweetener and flavouring. It acts
in a similar way to the hormone
insulin by helping to balance
blood sugar levels, making it a
natural aid for diabetics.

apple, cinnamon & raisin porridge

Porridge is a healthy way to start the day.
Packed with soluble fibre, oats are excellent
for improving digestion.

115g/4oz/heaped 1 cup Scotch
  oats
300ml/10½fl oz/1¼ cups milk or
  soya milk

2 apples, peeled, cored and
  chopped
1 tsp ground cinnamon
55g/2oz/½ cup raisins

1 Put the oats, milk, apples and cinnamon in a saucepan
over a medium heat and bring to the boil. Reduce
the heat and simmer gently, stirring occasionally, for
4–5 minutes until the mixture thickens and the oats
soften. Alternatively, put the ingredients in a micro-
wavable bowl and heat, covered, on high for 5 minutes,
stirring halfway through.
2 Spoon the porridge into bowls, scatter over the raisins
and serve immediately.

(V)

millet hot cakes

These hearty cakes make a healthy, satisfying breakfast and are equally delicious as a teatime treat. Serve hot with fresh or poached fruit or, if you are feeling really indulgent, drizzle some maple syrup over the top.

225g/8oz/2 cups millet
600ml/21fl oz/2½ cups apple juice
115g/4oz/scant 1 cup raisins
1 tsp ground cinnamon

1 tbsp rice flour, plus extra for rolling
150g/5½oz silken tofu
1 tbsp olive oil

1 Put the millet and apple juice in a pan and bring to the boil. Reduce the heat and simmer gently for 25 minutes. Add the raisins and cook for 5 minutes more.
2 Tip the mixture into the bowl of a food processor and add the cinnamon, rice flour and tofu. Process briefly to form a soft dough. Transfer the dough to a lightly floured surface and roll out to about 2.5cm/1in thick. Using an 6cm/2½in round pastry cutter, cut out 12 cakes.
3 Heat the oil in a large frying pan and fry the cakes, in batches, for 5 minutes on each side until golden. Leave to cool slightly, then serve.

SERVES 4

PREPARATION + COOKING
10 + 55 minutes

STORAGE
Make in advance and keep in the fridge for up to 3 days or freeze for up to 1 month. Warm through in the oven before serving.

SERVE THIS WITH...
Cranberry & Cherry Compote (see page 25)
natural or soya yogurt

HEALTH BENEFITS
Millet is a nutritious, gluten-free grain and a good source of protein. Rich in calcium, magnesium, potassium and B vitamins, it is a wonderful stress-busting food. It is also highly alkaline and full of fibre, so it can improve digestion and help lower cholesterol levels.

Ⓥ Ⓞ ⊚ ⊛

lemon buckwheat blinis

PREPARATION + COOKING
10 + 15 minutes

STORAGE
Make in advance and keep in the fridge for up to 3 days or freeze for up to 1 month. To reheat, preheat the oven to 190°C/375°F/ Gas 5. Put the blinis on a baking sheet, cover with foil and bake for 5 minutes until hot.

SERVE THIS WITH...
Cranberry & Cherry Compote (see page 25)
natural or soya yogurt with fresh or poached fruit

HEALTH BENEFITS
Despite its name, buckwheat isn't a grain but a fruit seed related to rhubarb. It contains all eight essential amino acids, making it a good source of protein. Rich in fibre and flavonoids, particularly rutin, it strengthens capillaries and helps detoxify the body.

These fabulous gluten-free blinis, flavoured with fresh lemon, are simple and quick to prepare. Make them dairy-free by replacing the milk with soya or rice milk.

100g/3½oz/¾ cup buckwheat
    flour
1 tsp gluten-free baking powder
2 tsp fructose
1 egg, separated

185ml/6fl oz/¾ cup milk
1 tbsp lemon juice
1 tsp grated lemon zest
1 tbsp olive oil

1 Put the buckwheat flour, baking powder, fructose, egg yolk, milk, lemon juice and zest in a bowl. Using a hand-held blender, blend until a smooth batter forms.
2 In a separate, clean bowl, whisk the egg white until stiff. Fold it into the batter.
3 Heat the oil in a large frying pan. Place 5 spoonfuls of the mixture in the pan, spacing well apart, and cook for 2–3 minutes on each side until golden. Remove the blinis from the pan and keep them warm while you cook the remaining batter. Serve warm.

Ⓥ Ⓞ Ⓕ Ⓖ Ⓒ Ⓧ

blueberry buttermilk pancakes

Processed pancake mixes can contain a lot of added salt. For the perfect leisurely breakfast, whip up a teetering stack of these thick, fluffy home-made pancakes instead.

100g/3½oz/²/₃ cup wholemeal
   flour
100g/3½oz/heaped ¾ cup plain
   flour
2 tsp baking powder
1 tbsp fructose

2 eggs, separated
250ml/9fl oz/1 cup buttermilk
   or natural yogurt
125g/4½oz/¾ cup blueberries
1 tbsp olive oil

1 Sift the flours, baking powder and fructose into a large bowl. In a separate bowl, mix together the egg yolks and buttermilk and add this mixture to the dry ingredients, stirring until the mixture forms a batter.
2 In another, clean bowl, whisk the egg whites until stiff. Fold them with the blueberries into the batter.
3 Heat the oil in a frying pan. Place about 5 spoonfuls of the batter in the pan, spacing well apart, and cook for 2–3 minutes on each side until golden. Remove the pancakes from the pan and keep them warm while you cook the remaining batter. Serve warm.

MAKES 8–12

PREPARATION + COOKING
10 + 15 minutes

STORAGE
Make in advance and keep in the fridge for up to 2 days or freeze for up to 1 month. To reheat, preheat the oven to 190°C/375°F/Gas 5. Put the pancakes on a baking sheet, cover with foil and bake for 5 minutes until hot.

SERVE THIS WITH...
Spicy Tomato Juice
  (see page 24)
fresh or poached berries
natural yogurt and maple syrup

HEALTH BENEFITS
Blueberries are a rich source of vitamin C and anthocyanins, the natural chemicals that give the fruit their intense colour. These potent chemicals protect the body against the effects of ageing, help strengthen blood capillaries and improve circulation.

HEALTH BENEFITS
A famous source of iron, spinach also contains other important nutrients, including calcium, magnesium and vitamin K for bone health. It is rich in vitamin C, which helps iron absorption, and in heart-friendly potassium, folic acid and vitamin B6.

*oat muffins with eggs & spinach

Poached eggs are a great comfort food. Teeming with protein, vitamins and minerals, they are also a great source of fuel to start the day. Combined here with savoury oat muffins and spinach, they make a perfect, energy-packed, low-salt breakfast.

olive oil, for greasing
150g/5½oz/1 cup self-raising wholemeal flour
½ tsp baking powder
55g/2oz/heaped ½ cup rolled oats
1 tsp thyme

2 eggs, beaten
150ml/5fl oz/⅔ cup milk or soya milk
200g/7oz baby spinach leaves
4 poached eggs, to serve
freshly ground black pepper

SERVES 4

PREPARATION + COOKING
15 + 20 minutes

STORAGE
The muffins can be made in advance and kept in an airtight container for up to 2 days or frozen for up to 1 month.

SERVE THIS WITH...
Mushroom & Garlic Medley (see page 39)
Pineapple, Lime & Avocado Smoothie (see page 23)

1 Preheat the oven to 220°C/425°F/Gas 7 and grease four holes of a muffin tin. Sift the flour and baking powder into a bowl and stir in the oats and thyme. Beat in the eggs and milk to form a batter.

2 Spoon the mixture into the tin and bake for 15 minutes until golden brown. Leave in the tin for 1 minute, then transfer to a wire rack to cool completely.

3 Put the spinach in a large saucepan over a medium heat and cook for 2–3 minutes, stirring occasionally, until just wilted. Split the muffins in half and toast them.

4 Top one half of each muffin with some of the spinach, followed by 1 poached egg. Sprinkle with black pepper and serve immediately.

> **Experiment with different fresh herbs, such as basil, sage and oregano, to give the oat muffins a bit of variety.**

SERVES 4

PREPARATION + COOKING
5 + 15 minutes

STORAGE
Make in advance and keep in the
fridge for up to 3 days.

SERVE THIS WITH…
Mushroom & Garlic Medley
 (see page 39)
Mediterranean Tortilla
 (see page 37)

HEALTH BENEFITS
Haricot beans provide plenty
of protein to help maintain
energy levels and fibre, which
is important for lowering blood
cholesterol and improving
digestion. They are also rich in
B vitamins, which help combat
stress and lower homocysteine
levels – a high amount of which
can increase risk of heart disease.

Ⓥ

baked beans

This home-made recipe is much healthier than
the shop-bought canned versions, which can
be high in salt, sugar and sweeteners. Use
tamari, a wheat-free, low-salt soy sauce, rather
than regular salty brands.

1 recipe quantity Tomato Sauce
 (see page 19)
400g/14oz canned haricot
 beans, no added salt or
 sugar, drained and rinsed
a pinch allspice

a pinch ground cinnamon
3 tbsp apple juice
2 tsp tamari
1 tsp cider vinegar
Oat Muffins (see page 34)
 or toast, to serve

1 Put all the ingredients in a saucepan and bring to the
boil. Reduce the heat and simmer gently for 15 minutes
until slightly thickened.
2 Serve with oat muffins or toast.

Ⓥ Ⓞ

mediterranean tortilla

This thick, Spanish-style omelette makes a hearty, protein-rich breakfast. It is also delicious cold, cut into wedges for packed lunches or picnics.

1 tbsp olive oil
1 small sweet potato, peeled and cut into small cubes
1 red onion, finely chopped
1 red pepper, deseeded and chopped

1 garlic clove, crushed
4 button mushrooms, sliced
1 handful basil, chopped
1 handful parsley, chopped
6 eggs, beaten
freshly ground black pepper

1 Heat the oil in an ovenproof frying pan. Add the potato and onion and cook for 5–6 minutes until the onion is soft. Add the pepper, garlic and mushrooms and cook for a further 5 minutes.

2 Preheat the grill to high. Stir the basil and parsley into the eggs and season to taste with black pepper. Pour the mixture over the vegetables in the pan, then reduce the heat and cook gently for 5–7 minutes, or until the eggs have almost set.

3 Place the pan under the grill and heat for 3–4 minutes until the top of the tortilla is golden brown. Cut into wedges and serve.

SERVES 4

PREPARATION + COOKING
10 + 25 minutes

STORAGE
Make in advance and keep in the fridge for up to 2 days.

SERVE THIS WITH...
Mango & Oat Smoothie (see page 22)
grilled tomatoes or Baked Beans (see page 36)

HEALTH BENEFITS
Eggs are an excellent source of protein, easily digestible and rich in the immune-boosting nutrients iron, zinc and selenium, as well as B vitamins for energy. Despite their image as a high-cholesterol food, they actually contain mostly monounsaturated fats, which help lower the risk of heart disease.

Ⓥ O

baked eggs with harissa

This luxurious breakfast treat is packed with antioxidants, making it incredibly nutritious.

STORAGE
Make the tomato mixture in advance and keep in the fridge for up to 2 days.

SERVE THIS WITH...
Pumpkin & Seed Bread (see page 79)
Pineapple, Lime & Avocado Smoothie (see page 23)

HEALTH BENEFITS
Chillies are potent immune-system boosters and effective natural painkillers – even in small quantities. They are also rich in beta-carotene – the antioxidant responsible for healthy skin and eyes – and the phytochemical capsaicin, which has natural analgesic properties that can help ease headaches, arthritis and sinusitis.

1 tbsp olive oil, plus extra for greasing
½ red onion, chopped
½ red pepper, deseeded and chopped
½ yellow pepper, deseeded and chopped
1 garlic clove, crushed
1 red chilli, deseeded and finely chopped
4 plum tomatoes, chopped
1 tsp harissa
4 eggs
1 tbsp chopped chives

1 Preheat the oven to 190°C/375°F/Gas 5 and grease four ramekins. Heat the oil in a frying pan, add the onion and peppers and cook over a low heat for 2–3 minutes until soft. Add the garlic, chilli, tomatoes and harissa and simmer for 10–15 minutes until the sauce is thick.
2 Spoon the mixture into the ramekins and make a slight depression on the top of the mixture. Break an egg into each ramekin. Put the ramekins in a roasting tin and pour enough hot water into the tin to come halfway up the sides of the ramekins.
3 Bake for 15–17 minutes until light brown on top. Sprinkle with chives and serve.

Ⓥ

mushroom & garlic medley

A fantastic flavouring to use instead of salt, garlic is a health-boosting superfood. It helps lower the body's levels of 'bad' cholesterol while boosting the 'good' cholesterol.

2 tbsp olive oil
2 garlic cloves, crushed
2 shallots, finely chopped

250g/9oz mixed mushrooms, such as shiitake, chestnut, portabellini and oyster, thickly sliced
2 tbsp chopped parsley
toast, to serve

1 Heat the oil in a large frying pan. Add the garlic and shallots and cook over a medium heat for 1–2 minutes until soft.
2 Add the mushrooms and stir-fry for 5–6 minutes until softened. Sprinkle with the parsley and serve on toast.

SERVES 4

PREPARATION + COOKING
5 + 8 minutes

STORAGE
Make in advance and keep in the fridge for up to 3 days.

SERVE THIS WITH...
Oat Muffins with Eggs & Spinach (see page 34)
Baked Beans (see page 36)
Pineapple, Lime & Avocado Smoothie (see page 23)

HEALTH BENEFITS
Mushrooms are a good source of B vitamins and the mineral selenium – an important antioxidant that supports immune function. Shiitake mushrooms contain active components like lentinan – a polysaccharide compound that helps lower cholesterol and fight cancer.

LUNCHES & SIDE DISHES

Shop-bought lunches like sandwiches, dips, pâtés and soups are notoriously high in salt, so making your own is one of the best ways to reduce your intake. By concentrating on the natural flavours of other ingredients – such as refreshing citrus, pungent sun-dried tomatoes, subtly bitter greens and fiery chillies – you can create delicious low-salt dishes that will quickly become favourites. From simple lunches to more leisurely meals, the recipes in this chapter are full of delicious ideas, such as Pesto Tuna Wraps and Thai-style Seared Beef & Spinach Salad, that will keep you sustained all afternoon.

017

roasted red pepper hummus

SERVES 4

PREPARATION
10 minutes

STORAGE
Make in advance and keep in the fridge for up to 1 week or freeze for up to 1 month.

SERVE THIS WITH...
Sun-dried Tomato Bread
(see page 80)
vegetable sticks, such as pepper,
cucumber and carrot;
mangetout and baby sweetcorn
Cherry & Ricotta Tarts
(see page 132)

HEALTH BENEFITS
Chickpeas are an excellent source of protein and soluble fibre, which helps balance blood sugar levels and lower cholesterol. They contain fructo-oligosaccharides, a type of fibre that helps support friendly bacteria in the gut, important for a healthy digestive system.

Home-made hummus is a breeze to make. This delicious version is packed with fibre, heart-healthy essential fatty acids and antioxidants – without the salt and saturated fat found in many shop-bought dips.

1 large Roasted Pepper (see page 19)	**1 tbsp lemon juice**
400g/14oz canned chickpeas, no added salt or sugar, drained and rinsed	**2 garlic cloves, crushed**
	1 tbsp tahini
	2 tbsp flaxseed or hemp oil
	a pinch paprika

1 Put the pepper, chickpeas, lemon juice, garlic and tahini in a food processor or blender. Blend for 3–4 minutes, or until the mixture forms a thick purée. Add the oil and process for a further 3–4 minutes until smooth and creamy.
2 Spoon the hummus into a bowl, sprinkle with the paprika and serve.

Ⓥ

sun-dried tomato dip

Sun-dried tomatoes give this dip a rich flavour without relying on processed salty sauces or pastes. Silken tofu is a great way to boost your intake of soya protein, which can help lower harmful cholesterol levels.

55g/2oz/⅓ cup sun-dried
  tomatoes
2 tsp low-salt sun-dried tomato
  paste
250g/9oz silken tofu
1 garlic clove, crushed

1 tbsp cider vinegar
1 tomato, deseeded and
  chopped
a few drops Tabasco sauce
a pinch cayenne pepper

1 Soak the sun-dried tomatoes in boiling water for 15 minutes, then drain and roughly chop them. Put them in a food processor with the tomato paste, tofu, garlic, vinegar and tomato. Blend for 3–4 minutes until smooth, then season to taste with the Tabasco sauce.
2 Spoon the dip into a bowl, sprinkle with the cayenne pepper and serve.

SERVES 4

PREPARATION
10 minutes + soaking

STORAGE
Make in advance and keep in the fridge for up to 4 days.

SERVE THIS WITH...
Spicy Tortilla Chips (see page 78)
  or plain oat cakes
vegetable sticks, such as carrot,
  pepper, cucumber and celery
fresh fruit
Apple Crunch Cake (see page 85)

HEALTH BENEFITS
Tofu is rich in protein and B vitamins, low in saturated fat and sodium and an important non-dairy source of calcium. Soya protein is great for the heart as it can lower cholesterol and triglyceride levels and reduce the likelihood of blood clots forming.

Ⓥ ☺

butternut squash & pear soup

This delightful soup combines antioxidant-rich vegetables with juicy pears. Full of antiviral and antibacterial properties, it is perfect for boosting your protection against infection.

SERVES 4

PREPARATION + COOKING
15 + 35 minutes

STORAGE
Make in advance and keep in the fridge for up to 3 days or freeze for up to 1 month.

SERVE THIS WITH…
Sun-dried Tomato Bread
  (see page 80)
low-salt cheese or lean turkey
Chocolate & Orange Soufflés
  (see page 133)
fresh fruit

HEALTH BENEFITS
Winter squashes and sweet potatoes are full of cancer-fighting, cardio-protective nutrients. They are rich in carotenoids and vitamins C and E – valuable antioxidants for skin, eyes, lungs and immune system. A great source of soluble fibre, they can help lower cholesterol and aid diestion.

2 tbsp olive oil
1 onion, chopped
300g/10½oz butternut squash, peeled, deseeded and chopped
1 sweet potato, peeled and chopped
3 pears, peeled, cored and chopped
¼ tsp garam masala
¼ tsp cayenne pepper
455ml/16fl oz/1¾ cups Home-made Vegetable Stock (see page 18)
5 tbsp low-fat crème fraîche
freshly ground black pepper

1 Heat the oil in a large saucepan. Add the onion and cook over a low heat for 3–4 minutes until softened.
2 Add the squash, potato, pears, spices and stock to the pan. Bring to the boil, then reduce the heat and simmer for 25 minutes or until the squash is tender.
3 Pour the soup into a food processor or blender and blend, in batches if necessary, until smooth. Return the soup to the rinsed pan, stir in the crème fraîche and season with pepper. Heat through gently and serve hot.

Ⓥ ⓑ

roasted garlic & tomato soup

Roasting the garlic and tomatoes lends this soup a rich, sweet flavour, and the beans and seeds provide valuable protein.

1 garlic bulb, cloves separated
  and peeled
2 tbsp olive oil
450g/1lb tomatoes, quartered
400g/14oz canned borlotti
  beans, no added salt or
  sugar, drained and rinsed

900ml/32fl oz/3²/₃ cups Home-
  made Vegetable Stock
  (see page 18)
1 tbsp lemon juice
1 tbsp chopped basil
2 tbsp pumpkin seeds, toasted
2 tbsp sunflower seeds, toasted

1 Preheat the oven to 200°C/400°F/Gas 6. Put the garlic in a roasting tin, drizzle with the oil and roast for 15 minutes until browned. Add the tomatoes to the garlic and cook for a further 10–15 minutes until the tomatoes are soft.
2 Tip the tomatoes and garlic into a blender. Add the beans and stock and blend for 2–3 minutes until smooth.
3 Pour the soup into a saucepan and stir in the lemon juice and basil. Reheat over a low heat, then ladle into bowls. Sprinkle with the seeds and serve immediately.

SERVES 4

PREPARATION + COOKING
10 + 35 minutes

STORAGE
Toast the seeds in advance and keep in an airtight container in the fridge for up to 1 week. Make the soup in advance and keep in the fridge for up to 3 days or freeze for up to 1 month.

SERVE THIS WITH...
Chilli Corn Muffins (see page 83)
Date & Lemon Oat Bars
  (see page 89)
fresh fruit and natural yogurt

HEALTH BENEFITS
Tomatoes are rich in lycopene, a natural plant compound that is best absorbed by the body when tomatoes are cooked. Lycopene has been shown to protect against cancer and guard the skin and eyes from sun damage.

021

Ⓥ

pea & lettuce soup

Lettuce contains a compound that relaxes the nervous system and relieves stress.

PREPARATION + COOKING
5 + 25 minutes

STORAGE
Make in advance and keep in the fridge for up to 4 days or freeze for up to 1 month.

SERVE THIS WITH...
Sesame Crackers (see page 76)
Pesto Tuna Wraps (see page 48)
Summer Berry Crisp
(see page 134)

HEALTH BENEFITS
Peas are a great heart-protecting food. Rich in folate and B vitamins, they can help lower homocysteine levels, a high level of which has been linked to heart disease. They also provide plenty of vitamin K, important for bone health and blood clotting.

1 tbsp olive oil
1 onion, finely chopped
1 celery stick
350g/12oz/2¼ cups frozen peas
2 Little Gem lettuces, roughly
    chopped

800ml/28floz/3¼ cups Home-
    made Vegetable Stock
    (see page 18)
juice of ½ lemon
1 tbsp chopped parsley
freshly ground black pepper

1 Heat the oil in a saucepan. Add the onion and celery and cook over a low heat for 5 minutes until tender.
2 Add the peas, lettuces and stock. Bring to the boil, then reduce the heat and simmer for 15 minutes until the peas are tender. Stir in the lemon juice and season with pepper.
3 Pour the soup into a food processor or blender. Add the parsley and blend, in batches if necessary, until smooth. Return the soup to the rinsed pan, reheat over a low heat and serve hot.

V

chilled pepper & bean soup with basil cream

This crimson-coloured soup is full of summer flavour and packed with healthy antioxidants.

1 tbsp olive oil
1 onion, finely chopped
1 garlic clove, crushed
600ml/21fl oz/2½ cups
  Home-made Vegetable
  Stock (see page 18)
a pinch chilli powder

3 Roasted Peppers
  (see page 19), chopped
400g/14oz canned cannellini
  beans, no added salt or
  sugar, drained and rinsed
1 handful basil
6 tbsp Greek yogurt

1 Heat the oil in a large saucepan. Add the onion and garlic and cook over a low heat for 5 minutes, then add the stock, chilli powder, peppers and beans. Bring to the boil, then reduce the heat and simmer, covered, for 15–20 minutes until the vegetables are tender.
2 Pour the soup into a food processor or blender and blend, in batches, until smooth. Place a sieve over a large bowl and strain the soup, using a wooden spoon to push it through the sieve. Cover and chill for 1 hour.
3 Put the basil and yogurt in a blender and blend for 1 minute until combined. Serve the chilled soup drizzled with the basil cream.

SERVES 4

PREPARATION + COOKING
10 + 25 minutes + chilling

STORAGE
Make the soup in advance and keep in the fridge for up to 3 days or freeze for up to 1 month. The basil cream will keep in the fridge for up to 2 days.

SERVE THIS WITH...
Sun-dried Tomato Bread
  (see page 80)
Cherry & Ricotta Tarts
  (see page 132)
fresh fruit

HEALTH BENEFITS
Red peppers contain more vitamin C than oranges – vital for a healthy immune system, lowering cholesterol levels and regulating blood pressure by thinning the blood. They also contain beta-carotene and flavonoids – potent antioxidants that strengthen blood capillaries and help fight disease.

023

SERVES 4

PREPARATION
15 minutes

STORAGE
The pesto can be made in
advance and kept in the fridge
for up to 1 week. The covered
wraps will keep in the fridge for
up to 2 days.

SERVE THIS WITH...
Summer Leaves with Mango
  Vinaigrette (see page 66)
Amaretto Biscotti (see page 90)
fresh fruit

HEALTH BENEFITS
Tuna is an excellent source of
protein and although canned
tuna lacks the omega-3 fats
found in fresh tuna, it still
provides useful amounts of
vitamins and minerals, including
B vitamins – important for
a healthy heart and nervous
system – and the antioxidant
selenium.

pesto tuna wraps

The pumpkin seed pesto in these nutritious
wraps is rich in heart-protecting omega-3 and
omega-6 essential fats. The pesto is extremely
versatile – add it to pasta, vegetables and
potato salads or use it as a dressing.

4 reduced-salt tortilla wraps
150g/5½oz canned tuna in
    water, drained and flaked
2 handfuls mixed salad leaves

Pumpkin Seed Pesto:
1 garlic clove, chopped
30g/1oz/¹/₃ cup basil
30g/1oz/¹/₃ cup pumpkin seeds
5 tbsp hemp oil or flaxseed oil
2 tbsp freshly grated Parmesan
    or Gruyère cheese

1 Put the garlic, basil and seeds in a food processor
and blend for 2–3 minutes until smooth. With the motor
running, add the oil in a thin stream to form a paste,
blending for a further 2 minutes. Stir in the cheese.
2 Spread each tortilla with 1 tbsp pesto and top with the
tuna and salad leaves. Roll tightly into wraps and serve.

lime & chilli turkey burrito

Lime and chilli give this dish a punchy flavour without adding salt. Turkey is a very lean meat that is rich in valuable B vitamins.

1 tbsp olive oil
3 turkey breasts, cut into
   thin strips
1 red chilli, deseeded and
   chopped
4 spring onions, chopped

juice and grated zest of 1 lime
4 reduced-salt tortilla wraps
1 handful rocket leaves
4 tbsp chopped coriander
   leaves
4 tbsp Greek yogurt

1 Preheat the oven to 200°C/400°F/Gas 6. Heat the oil in a frying pan, add the turkey and chilli and stir-fry for about 5 minutes until the turkey is cooked. Add the spring onions and lime and cook for a further 1 minute.
2 Cut out four pieces of foil, each one large enough to completely wrap a tortilla. Put one tortilla on each piece of foil and top with the cooked turkey. Fold the foil over the tortillas to cover and place the foil packages on a baking sheet. Bake for 5–6 minutes until heated through.
3 Remove the foil and sprinkle the tortillas with the rocket leaves, coriander leaves and yogurt. Roll up and serve.

SERVES 4

PREPARATION + COOKING
10 + 12 minutes

STORAGE
The turkey can be prepared the day before and kept in the fridge overnight. Spoon it over the tortillas and warm through for 10 minutes in the oven.

SERVE THIS WITH...
Asian Coleslaw (see page 67)
Mango & Coconut Tray Bake
   (see page 88)
fresh fruit

HEALTH BENEFITS
Packed with vitamin C, limes are a real boost to the immune system. They also contain potassium, to counter excess sodium intake and balance fluid levels, and limonene, which supports the liver and digestion.

chicken rice paper wraps

HEALTH BENEFITS
Chicken is an excellent low-fat source of protein and it is full of B vitamins – vital for a healthy nervous system, energy production and preventing cardiovascular disease. It is also rich in the antioxidant selenium and the mineral potassium, which is useful for lowering high blood pressure.

Rice paper wrappers are ideal for anyone with a wheat or gluten sensitivity – and they are a great low-salt option. The tangy garlic and chilli sauce is salt-free and incredibly versatile. Protein-rich foods, such as chicken, are more satisfying and filling and help prevent mid-afternoon energy slumps.

20 rice paper wrappers
400g/14oz roast chicken, cut
    into long strips
4 spring onions, finely sliced
1 carrot, peeled and cut into
    matchsticks
½ red pepper, deseeded and
    cut into thin strips
1 handful bean sprouts

Garlic & Chilli Sauce:
2 tbsp rice wine vinegar
3 tbsp honey
1 shallot, chopped
1 red chilli, finely chopped
4 garlic cloves, crushed
3 tomatoes, chopped

MAKES 10

PREPARATION + COOKING
30 + 15 minutes

STORAGE
Make the wraps in advance and
keep in the fridge, covered, for
up to 2 days. The garlic and chilli
sauce can be kept in the fridge
for up to 1 week.

SERVE THIS WITH...
Asian Coleslaw (see page 67)
Tropical Fruit Skewers
    (see page 139)

1 To make the sauce, put all the ingredients in a saucepan,
bring to the boil and then reduce the heat. Simmer gently
for 10–12 minutes until the mixture begins to thicken.
Blend, using an electric hand-held blender, until smooth.
2 Soak 2 rice paper wrappers in warm water for 1–2
minutes until pliable and opaque. Place them on top of
each other on a chopping board. Spread 1 tsp of the
sauce over the top wrapper, then top with a few strips of
chicken and vegetables. Roll both wrappers up together,
folding in the edges as you roll. Repeat with the remaining
wrappers and filling to make 10 wraps.
3 Serve the wraps with the remaining sauce for dipping.

Make up a large
batch of the garlic and
chilli sauce and use it
to coat meats or as an
accompaniment
to cheese.

Ⓥ Ⓞ Ⓞ Ⓞ Ⓞ Ⓞ

SERVES 4

PREPARATION + COOKING
10 + 5 minutes

STORAGE
This is best assembled just
before eating.

SERVE THIS WITH...
Summer Leaves with Mango
  Vinaigrette (see page 66)
Asparagus & Herb Frittata
  (see page 54)
Lemon-Berry Cheesecake
  (see page 130)

HEALTH BENEFITS
Avocados are loaded with
heart-healthy monounsaturated
fat, fibre, vitamin E, folic acid
and iron. They also contain
beta-sitosterol, a substance that
protects against cancer and can
reduce cholesterol. Avocados
are one of the richest sources
of potassium, essential for
balancing body fluids.

avocado & tomato bruschetta

A popular Italian starter or snack, bruschetta
makes a healthy lunch choice, especially when
topped with super-nutritious avocado.

2 garlic cloves
1 avocado, peeled, stoned
  and chopped
1 tomato, chopped
1 tbsp chopped basil

3 tbsp olive oil
1 tbsp balsamic vinegar
4 slices Sun-dried Tomato
  Bread (see page 80)

1 Crush one of the garlic cloves and put it in a bowl
with the avocado, tomato, basil, 2 tbsp of the oil and the
vinegar. Stir carefully to combine.
2 Heat a griddle pan until hot, then add the slices of bread
and toast them on both sides. Rub the toasted bread with
the remaining garlic clove and drizzle with the remaining
oil. Spoon the avocado mixture onto the bread and serve.

V / / /

artichoke & onion tarts

These little tarts use reduced-salt wholemeal bread, rather than pastry or regular bread. Artichokes and onions are good sources of potassium to help balance fluid levels and regulate blood pressure.

8 thin slices low-salt
   wholemeal bread
2 tbsp olive oil
½ red onion, chopped
1 garlic clove, crushed

225g/8oz canned artichoke
   hearts in water, drained and
   chopped
3 tbsp grated Gruyère cheese
3 tbsp low-fat crème fraîche
1 tbsp chopped basil

1 Preheat the oven to 200°C/400°F/Gas 6. Using an 8cm/3in pastry cutter, stamp out 8 circles from the bread. Drizzle 1 tbsp of the oil over the 8 circles, then press each one into a hole in a shallow muffin tin.
2 Heat the remaining oil in a small frying pan, add the onion and garlic and cook over a medium heat for 2–3 minutes until soft. Tip the onions into a bowl and stir in the artichokes, cheese, crème fraîche and basil. Spoon the mixture into the bread cases.
3 Bake for 15–20 minutes until golden. Serve warm.

MAKES 8/SERVES 8

PREPARATION + COOKING
10 + 25 minutes

STORAGE
Make in advance and keep in the fridge for up to 3 days.

SERVE THIS WITH...
Balsamic-roasted Beetroot
   (see page 68)
Summer Leaves with Mango
   Vinaigrette (see page 66)
Date & Lemon Oat Bars
   (see page 89)
fresh fruit

HEALTH BENEFITS
Cheese is an excellent source of calcium for strong bones and teeth, but be careful which cheese you choose because many of them are high in salt. Gruyère, Emmental, mozzarella and ricotta are some of the best low-salt options, or look for reduced-salt versions of your favourites.

asparagus & herb frittata

This nutritious Italian-style omelette is delicious hot or cold and is great for picnics.

SERVES 6

PREPARATION + COOKING
10 + 20 minutes

STORAGE
Leftovers can be kept in the fridge for up to 3 days.

SERVE THIS WITH...
Balsamic-roasted Beetroot
  (see page 68)
Summer Leaves with Mango
  Vinaigrette (see page 66)
Summer Berry Crisp
  (see page 134)

HEALTH BENEFITS
Asparagus contains the alkaloid asparagine, which stimulates the kidneys and has a strong diuretic effect. Its cleansing properties help combat fluid retention. It is also a good source of folate, beta-carotene, vitamin C and the antioxidant glutathione, which can all help reduce the risk of heart disease.

2 tbsp olive oil
4 new potatoes, scrubbed and
   sliced into 5mm/¼in rounds
1 onion, chopped

350g/12oz asparagus,
   char-grilled and sliced
3 tbsp chopped chives
6 eggs, beaten

1 Heat 1 tbsp of the oil in an ovenproof frying pan. Add the potatoes and cook over a high heat, stirring occasionally until just soft, about 5 minutes. Add the onion and cook for a further 2–3 minutes until soft. Tip into a bowl and stir in the asparagus, chives and eggs.
2 Preheat the grill to high. Heat the remaining oil in the pan, pour in the egg mixture and cook over a low heat until the top has almost set, about 10 minutes.
3 Put the pan under the grill and cook for about 2 minutes until the top is golden brown. Cut into wedges and serve.

sweetcorn & pepper fritters

These tasty fritters are sure to be a hit with the whole family – and are a great way of boosting your intake of antioxidant rich vegetables.

175g/6oz/scant 1½ cups wholemeal self-raising flour
1 tsp baking powder
2 eggs
125ml/4fl oz/½ cup milk or soya milk

225g/8oz canned sweetcorn, no added salt or sugar, drained
1 Roasted Pepper (see page 19), chopped
2 spring onions, chopped
1 tbsp chopped parsley
1 tbsp olive oil

1 Put the flour, baking powder, eggs and milk in a bowl. Mix for 1–2 minutes, using a hand-held electric mixer, until the mixture forms a smooth batter. Stir in the sweetcorn, pepper, spring onions and parsley.
2 Heat the oil in a frying pan over a medium heat until hot. Place 5 tbsp of the batter in the pan, spacing well apart. Reduce the heat and cook for 1–2 minutes on each side until golden. Remove the fritters from the pan and keep them warm while you cook the rest of the mixture in the same way. Serve warm.

MAKES 10–12/ SERVES 4

PREPARATION + COOKING
10 + 15 minutes

STORAGE
Make in advance and keep in the fridge for up to 3 days. To reheat, cover with foil and bake at 190°C/375°F/Gas 5 for 5 minutes.

SERVE THIS WITH...
Citrus, Bean Sprout & Avocado Salad (see page 63)
lean turkey
Fruit & Seed Tea Bread (see page 84)
fresh fruit

HEALTH BENEFITS
Sweetcorn contains plenty of immune-boosting vitamin C and fibre for lowering blood cholesterol. It also provides folate and B vitamins, important for boosting energy and combating stress.

SERVES 4

PREPARATION + COOKING
10 + 10 minutes + marinating

STORAGE
Make the dressing in advance
and keep in the fridge for up to
1 week. Get ahead by marinating
the salmon in the morning and
storing it in the fridge until ready
to cook.

SERVE THIS WITH...
Sun-dried Tomato Bread
  (see page 80)
Amaretto Biscotti (see page 90)
fresh fruit and yogurt

HEALTH BENEFITS
Eating more beans and pulses
is a great way of boosting your
health. High in soluble fibre, they
fill you up, stabilize blood sugar
levels and help lower cholesterol.
They are also rich in potassium
to help balance body fluids
and in homocysteine-lowering
B vitamins and folate.

pan-fried salmon with tomato & bean salad

Salmon is an excellent source of omega-3 fatty acids, which can help prevent heart disease.

juice and grated zest
  of ½ lemon
2 tbsp rice vinegar
2 tbsp mirin
2 tbsp olive oil
4 salmon fillets, about 150g/
  5½oz each
2 garlic cloves, crushed

250g/9oz cherry tomatoes,
  halved
400g/14oz canned mixed
  beans, no added salt or
  sugar, drained and rinsed
2 tbsp chopped mint

1 Whisk together the lemon juice and zest, vinegar, mirin and 1 tbsp of the oil. Spoon half this dressing over the salmon and leave to stand for 15 minutes.

2 Heat the remaining oil in a frying pan. Add the fish and cook over a high heat for 2–3 minutes on each side until cooked through; remove it from the pan and set aside.

3 Add the garlic to the pan and cook over a low heat for 2 minutes. Add the tomatoes and beans and cook for 2–3 minutes until the tomatoes start to soften. Add the remaining dressing and cook for 1 minute until heated through. Sprinkle with the mint and serve with the fish.

coconut, prawn & papaya salad

The coconut in this healthy Thai-inspired salad contains medium-chain triglycerides and manganese to help burn calories and boost energy.

50g/2oz creamed coconut, grated
125ml/4fl oz/½ cup natural yogurt
juice of ½ lemon
a pinch chilli powder
2 spring onions, chopped
200g/7oz cooked king prawns

1 avocado, peeled, stoned and sliced
4 handfuls mixed salad leaves
1 papaya, peeled, deseeded and sliced
toasted unsweetened coconut flakes, to serve
coriander leaves, to serve

1 Put the coconut in a heatproof bowl, pour over 2 tbsp boiling water and leave to cool. Stir in the yogurt, lemon juice, chilli powder and spring onions.
2 Put the prawns and avocado in a bowl, pour over the coconut dressing and toss gently.
3 Divide the salad leaves on to four serving plates, then spoon over the prawn mixture and top with the slices of papaya. Sprinkle with the coconut flakes and coriander leaves and serve.

SERVES 4

PREPARATION
15 minutes

STORAGE
This salad is best eaten the day it is made.

SERVE THIS WITH...
Spiced Flatbreads (see page 82)
Spice-poached Pears
(see page 135)

HEALTH BENEFITS
Papaya is a wonderful digestive aid thanks to a powerful enzyme called papain, which helps break down proteins. The fruit is soothing for the gut and, being rich in fibre, it helps control cholesterol levels and relieve constipation. It is also full of skin-friendly beta-carotene.

032

crab & fennel salad

Crab is so flavourful there is no need to smother it in creamy, salty dressings. Cucumber is a great diuretic – useful for keeping blood pressure down.

SERVES 4

PREPARATION
15 minutes

STORAGE
Make the dressing in advance and keep in the fridge for up to 2 days.

SERVE THIS WITH...
Sesame Crackers (see page 76)
Orange & Cranberry Muffins
  (see page 86)
fresh fruit and yogurt

HEALTH BENEFITS
Watercress is packed with antioxidants, including lutein and zeaxanthin for eye health, anti-cancer glucosinolates and the powerful anti-inflammatory quercetin. It also contains plenty of vitamin C, iron, folic acid and vitamin B6, needed to make healthy red blood cells and support the immune system.

½ cucumber, deseeded and
  sliced
1 fennel bulb, cored and thinly
  sliced
100g/3½oz watercress
500g/1lb 2oz white crab meat
freshly ground black pepper

Lemon & Ginger Dressing:
juice and grated zest of
  ½ lemon
1 tsp clear honey
1 tbsp extra virgin olive oil
1 tsp grated root ginger
1 tbsp chopped mint

1 Put all the dressing ingredients in a small bowl and whisk well.
2 Put the cucumber, fennel and watercress in a large bowl, pour over the dressing and toss.
3 Season the crab with black pepper and add it to the salad, then serve.

chicken & artichoke salad

This nutty, subtly sweet vinaigrette supplies plenty of heart-protecting omega fats. The chicken and walnuts are good sources of protein, selenium and vitamin E for healthy skin and heart.

2 handfuls rocket leaves
2 handfuls lamb's lettuce or
    baby spinach leaves
3 roasted chicken breasts,
    shredded
400g/14oz canned artichoke
    hearts in water, drained and
    halved

1 small red onion, chopped
6 cherry tomatoes, halved
100g/3½oz/1 cup walnut
    pieces, toasted

Walnut Vinaigrette:
3 tbsp sherry vinegar
5 tbsp walnut oil
1 tbsp extra virgin olive oil

1 Put all the dressing ingredients in a small bowl and whisk well.

2 Arrange the rocket and lamb's lettuce on a large serving platter. Scatter over the chicken, artichokes, onion, tomatoes and walnuts. Drizzle the dressing over the top and serve immediately.

SERVES 4

PREPARATION
15 minutes

STORAGE
Make the dressing the day before and keep it in the fridge overnight.

SERVE THIS WITH...
Sun-dried Tomato Bread
    (see page 80)
Apple Crunch Cake (see page 85)
fresh fruit

HEALTH BENEFITS
Artichokes contain cynarin, a compound that supports the liver, boosting detoxification and digestion. They are also a useful diuretic and can help relieve water retention and regulate blood pressure.

*seared beef & spinach salad

HEALTH BENEFITS
Lean beef is an excellent source of iron, which is needed for the manufacture of red blood cells, as well as zinc, for a healthy immune system. Beef also provides plenty of protein, which is great for giving you an energy boost if you're beginning to flag.

This low-salt, Thai-style salad features a rainbow selection of crunchy vegetables and spinach. It provides a wealth of powerful antioxidants and nutrients to help fight disease.

500g/1lb 2oz sirloin steak
1 tbsp olive oil
2 tbsp crushed black
    peppercorns
1 carrot, cut into matchsticks
1 red pepper, cut into
    matchsticks
1 red onion, thinly sliced

½ cucumber, deseeded and
    cut into matchsticks
1 recipe quantity Asian-style
    Vinaigrette (see page 18)
1 large handful baby spinach
4 tbsp chopped coriander
    leaves

SERVES 4

PREPARATION + COOKING
10 + 10 minutes + marinating

STORAGE
The dressing can be made in
advance and kept in the fridge
for up to 1 week.

1 Rub the steaks all over with the oil and peppercorns.
Leave to marinate for 1 hour.

2 Heat a frying pan over a high heat until hot. Cook each
side of the steak for 1 minute until brown, then reduce the
heat and cook for 3–4 minutes on each side until the meat
is cooked but still tender. Remove the steak from the pan,
leave it to rest for 10 minutes, then slice it very thinly.

3 Put the sliced steak in a bowl and add the carrot,
pepper, onion and cucumber. Pour the vinaigrette over
and toss well.

4 Put the spinach on a large platter and top with the
beef salad. Sprinkle with the coriander leaves and
serve immediately.

SERVE THIS WITH...
egg or soba noodles
Tropical Fruit Skewers
    (see page 139)

For a lunchbox,
pack the dressing
separately and add it
right before eating so
that the spinach and
other vegetables
stay crisp.

Ⓥ ⊘

fruity quinoa salad

This salad features a stellar array of flavours and textures, which means there's no need to add salt. Dubbed the 'supergrain', quinoa is an excellent protein-rich, gluten-free food.

SERVES 4–6

PREPARATION + COOKING
10 + 25 minutes

STORAGE
Leftover salad can be stored in the fridge for up to 3 days.

SERVE THIS WITH...
Summer Leaves with Mango Vinaigrette (see page 66)
Date & Lemon Oat Bars (see page 89)
fresh fruit and yogurt

HEALTH BENEFITS
Quinoa is an incredibly nutritious grain, providing plenty of calcium, phosphorus, iron, B vitamins and vitamin E. Its high fibre content can aid digestion, relieve constipation and lower cholesterol levels.

175g/6oz/heaped ¾ cup quinoa
500ml/17fl oz/2 cups Home-made Vegetable Stock (see page 18)
2 tbsp olive oil
1 red onion, finely chopped
1 tbsp ground cumin
1 tbsp ground coriander
1 apple, peeled and finely chopped
½ red pepper, deseeded and finely chopped
55g/2oz/¹/₃ cup unsalted, roasted cashew nuts
55g/2oz/½ cup raisins
55g/2oz/¹/₃ cup dried apricots, chopped
2 tbsp chopped coriander leaves

1 Put the quinoa and vegetable stock in a pan. Bring to the boil, then reduce the heat, cover and simmer gently for 15–20 minutes until the water has been absorbed. Remove from the heat and leave to cool.
2 Heat the oil in a pan, add the onion and spices and cook over a medium heat for 2–3 minutes until the onion is soft. Tip the onion mixture into the quinoa, then add the apple, pepper, nuts, raisins, apricots and coriander. Toss well and serve at room temperature.

Ⓥ ⊗ ⊙

citrus, bean sprout & avocado salad

Citrus fruits, avocado and crunchy bean sprouts are teamed here in a delicious salad that is packed with vitamin C and essential fatty acids to help boost the immune system.

2 avocados, peeled, stoned
  and sliced
1 grapefruit, peeled and sliced
1 orange, peeled and sliced
1 red onion, finely chopped
1 large handful mixed bean
  sprouts, such as mung
  beans and alfalfa sprouts

Dressing:
3 tbsp orange juice
2 tbsp hemp or flaxseed oil
1 garlic clove, crushed
1 tsp honey
2 tbsp white wine vinegar

1 Put all the dressing ingredients in a screw-top jar, seal and shake well.

2 Put the avocados, grapefruit, orange, onion and bean sprouts in a large bowl. Pour the dressing over the top and toss gently to coat. Serve immediately.

SERVES 4

PREPARATION
10 minutes

STORAGE
Make the dressing in advance and keep in the fridge for up to 4 days. The salad is best eaten as soon as possible.

SERVE THIS WITH...
Pesto Tuna Wraps (see page 48)
Cranberry & Date Balls
  (see page 91)
fresh fruit

HEALTH BENEFITS
Sprouted beans and seeds are nutritional stars. Concentrated sources of phytonutrients, protein, vitamins and minerals, they are fantastic energy and immune boosters. Rich in enzymes, they are easily digestible, enabling our bodies to break down and absorb the nutrients. Eat them raw in salads or sandwiches to maximize their nutritional benefits.

spicy stir-fried prawns

SERVES 4

PREPARATION + COOKING
10 + 5 minutes + marinating

STORAGE
Make the day before and keep
in the fridge overnight.

SERVE THIS WITH...
Spiced Flatbreads (see page 82)
Asian Coleslaw (see page 67)
Mango & Coconut Tray Bake
   (see page 88)
fresh fruit

HEALTH BENEFITS
Prawns are an excellent source
of minerals, including zinc, an
important immune booster, and
selenium, an antioxidant that
assists in the production of
antibodies. They also contain
B vitamins, calcium, magnesium
and potassium.

This simple, speedy lunch can be assembled in
the morning and left to marinate in the fridge
to allow the prawns to absorb the flavour of
the spices. A great protein dish, it will keep
you focused and energized all afternoon.

450g/1lb large raw prawns,
   peeled and deveined
4 tbsp Greek yogurt
2 tbsp lemon juice
1 garlic clove, crushed
1 tsp paprika

1 tsp garam masala
½ tsp ground cumin
½ tsp ground coriander
1 tbsp olive oil
1 tbsp chopped coriander
   leaves

1 Put the prawns, yogurt, lemon juice, garlic and
spices in a bowl and stir well. Cover and chill for at
least 30 minutes to let the flavours develop.
2 Heat the oil in a frying pan. Drain the prawns and
add them to the pan. Stir-fry the prawns over a high
heat for 3–4 minutes until pink and cooked through.
Sprinkle with the coriander leaves and serve.

lemon chicken & asparagus linguine

Citrus fruit like lemons and limes are a great way of flavouring food instead of using salt.

1 tbsp olive oil
1 garlic clove, crushed
2 shallots, finely chopped
400g/14oz chicken fillets, cut
    into bite-sized pieces
250g/9oz asparagus tips,
    halved lengthways

juice and grated zest of
    1 lemon
400g/14oz linguine
4 tbsp low-fat crème fraîche
30g/1oz/¹/₃ cup chopped basil

1 Heat the oil in a frying pan over a low heat. Add the garlic and shallots and cook for 2 minutes until they begin to soften. Add the chicken and cook for 7–8 minutes, stirring occasionally, until golden.

2 Meanwhile, bring a pan of water to the boil, add the linguine and cook according to the packet instructions until al dente, about 8 minutes. Drain well.

3 Add the asparagus, lemon juice and zest to the chicken and cook for a further 3–4 minutes until the asparagus is tender. Add the linguine, crème fraîche and basil. Toss well, heat through and serve immediately.

SERVES 4

PREPARATION + COOKING
10 + 20 minutes

STORAGE
Any leftovers will keep in the fridge for up to 2 days.

SERVE THIS WITH...
mixed salad
Lemon-Berry Cheesecake
(see page 130)

HEALTH BENEFITS
Lemons are an excellent source of immune-boosting vitamin C and antioxidants that help protect the body from damaging free radicals associated with ageing. They are also a wonderful cleansing food – begin the day with a glass of hot water and lemon juice to kick-start your digestion.

039

PREPARATION
15 minutes

STORAGE:
Make the dressing in advance
and keep it in the fridge for up
to 3 days.

SERVE THIS WITH...
Artichoke & Onion Tarts
  (see page 53)
Summer Berry Crisp
  (see page 134)

HEALTH BENEFITS
The mango's gorgeous orange-
yellow colour highlights their
beta-carotene content, important
for healthy skin and immune
system. They also provide
plenty of vitamin C, vitamin
E and potassium – good for
strengthening blood vessels
and protecting the heart.

summer leaves with mango vinaigrette

This delicious, refreshing salad is tossed in
a fruity dressing bursting with antioxidants and
essential fatty acids. Include a variety of salad
leaves for maximum nutrition.

300g/10½oz mixed salad
  leaves
1 mango, peeled, stoned
  and sliced
1 small red onion, finely
  chopped
½ cucumber, deseeded and
  sliced

Mango Vinaigrette:
1 mango, peeled, stoned
  and sliced
juice and grated zest of 1 lemon
1 garlic clove, crushed
1 tsp honey
2 tbsp raspberry vinegar
3 tbsp flaxseed or hemp oil

1 Put all the vinaigrette ingredients in a blender and blend
for 2–3 minutes until smooth.
2 Put the salad leaves, mango, onion and cucumber in
a bowl. Pour the dressing over the top and toss gently
to mix. Serve immediately.

asian coleslaw

Most mayonnaise-based sauces are high in saturated fat and salt. The Asian-inspired dressing used here features a number of flavourful exotic spices that are enriched with a little heart-healthy olive oil. This coleslaw makes a delicious accompaniment to grilled meats and fish or spicy burgers.

1 tbsp extra virgin olive oil
1 recipe quantity Asian-style Vinaigrette (see page 18)
200g/7oz red cabbage, finely shredded

2 carrots, peeled and grated
1 red pepper, deseeded and thinly sliced
100g/3½oz bean sprouts
4 spring onions, thinly sliced

1 Stir the olive oil into the vinaigrette.
2 Put the cabbage, carrot, pepper, bean sprouts and spring onions in a serving bowl and toss to mix. Pour the vinaigrette over the top, leave to stand for 15 minutes and then serve.

SERVES 4

PREPARATION
15 minutes

STORAGE
Make in advance and keep in the fridge for up to 4 days.

SERVE THIS WITH...
Thai Crab Cakes (see page 97)
Mango & Coconut Tray Bake (see page 88)
fresh fruit

HEALTH BENEFITS
Cabbage contains a range of powerful sulphurous substances, including glucosinolates that help protect against certain cancers and enhance the liver's detoxing capacity. It is also rich in vitamin C, fibre, folic acid and potassium – all valuable nutrients for maintaining a healthy heart.

Ⓥ

balsamic-roasted beetroot

Forget pickled beetroot – fresh roasted beetroot has an incomparable sweet, earthy flavour that doesn't need to be loaded down with salt. A great blood purifier, it also contains a wealth of powerful antioxidants.

SERVES 4

PREPARATION + COOKING
10 + 40 minutes

STORAGE
The beetroot can be cooked in advance and served hot or cold. Keep leftovers in the fridge for up to 3 days.

SERVE THIS WITH...
Baked Sesame Trout
  (see page 102)
Orange-Honey Sweet Potatoes
  (see page 71)
Lemon-Berry Cheesecake
  (see page 130)

HEALTH BENEFITS
Beetroot is a great cleansing food and can boost the liver's detoxifying properties. Rich in soluble fibre, it can also help lower cholesterol. Being naturally high in sugars and iron, beetroot keeps you feeling energized and boosts concentration.

8 baby beetroot or 4 medium
  beetroot, peeled
3 tbsp balsamic vinegar
4 tbsp olive oil

juice of ½ orange
1 garlic clove, crushed
1 tsp chopped rosemary
freshly ground black pepper

1 Preheat the oven to 200°C/400°F/Gas 6. Cut the medium beetroot, if using, in half. Put a sheet of foil on a baking sheet and arrange the beetroot on top.
2 Put the remaining ingredients in a bowl and whisk well. Drizzle the mixture over the beetroot, then gather up the foil to form a parcel and seal. Roast for 40 minutes until the beetroot is tender, then serve.

V ⊘ ⊛

mint & lemon courgettes

The lemon dressing in this summery dish is a great alternative to salt and can be paired with other grilled or steamed vegetables. Using flaxseed or hemp oil is a good way to get healthy omega fats into your diet.

4 courgettes, thinly sliced
  lengthways
1 tbsp olive oil
freshly ground black pepper

Lemon & Mint Dressing:
2 tbsp lemon juice
1 tsp grated lemon zest
2 tsp honey
4 tbsp hemp or flaxseed oil
1 handful mint, chopped

1 Put all the ingredients for the dressing in a bowl and whisk well.
2 Put the courgettes in another bowl and drizzle with the olive oil, then season with black pepper.
3 Heat a griddle or frying pan until hot and cook the courgettes, in batches, for 2–3 minutes on each side until golden brown.
4 Put the griddled courgettes in a clean bowl, pour the dressing over while they are still warm and toss gently. Serve warm or at room temperature.

SERVES 4

PREPARATION + COOKING
10 + 20 minutes

STORAGE
Leftovers will keep in the fridge for up to 2 days.

SERVE THIS WITH...
Lamb Koftas with Mint Yogurt
  (see page 114)
wholemeal pitta bread
Cherry & Ricotta Tarts
  (see page 132)

HEALTH BENEFITS
Peppermint contains menthol, a volatile oil that is useful for clearing congestion. It also promotes the secretion of digestive juices and has calming and anti-inflammatory properties to soothe an irritable bowel.

SERVES 4

PREPARATION + COOKING
10 + 10 minutes

STORAGE
Best eaten immediately.

SERVE THIS WITH...
Vietnamese Pork Noodles
  (see page 112)
Tropical Fruit Skewers
  (see page 139)

HEALTH BENEFITS
Broccoli is a superfood for the
heart and immune system.
It is an excellent source of
antioxidants and fibre to help
lower cholesterol. It is also high
in folate, which is useful for
reducing levels of homocysteine
in the blood. Like other
cruciferous vegetables, it
contains glucosinolates, which
have powerful detoxifying and
anti-cancer properties.

chilli & sesame broccoli

Stir-frying vegetables is a great way of retaining
their nutrients and maximizing their natural
flavours without adding salt. Sesame seeds
increase the protein content of this dish
and provide health-promoting omega-6 and
omega-9 fatty acids.

3 tsp sesame seeds
2 tbsp olive oil
1 shallot, finely chopped
1 red chilli, deseeded and
  finely chopped

2 garlic cloves, crushed
450g/1lb broccoli, cut into
  small florets
toasted sesame oil, to serve

1 Heat a non-stick pan over a medium heat until hot. Add
the sesame seeds and toast for 1–2 minutes until golden.
Watch them carefully so they do not burn. Remove from
the heat and set aside.

2 Heat the olive oil in a large frying pan over a low heat.
Add the shallot, chilli and garlic and cook for 2–3 minutes
until softened.

3 Add the broccoli and 1 tbsp water and stir-fry for 3–4
minutes until just soft. Scatter over the toasted sesame
seeds, drizzle with sesame oil and serve.

Ⓥ ⓣ

honey-orange sweet potatoes

Incredibly nutrient-rich, sweet potatoes are digested more slowly than other potatoes, helping to maintain energy levels for longer.

2 tbsp olive oil
2 tbsp honey
3 tbsp orange juice

4 sweet potatoes, peeled and cut into wedges
freshly ground black pepper

1 Preheat the oven to 200°C/400°F/Gas 6. Put the oil, honey and orange juice in a small bowl and season to taste with black pepper. Whisk well.
2 Put the sweet potatoes in a roasting tin, pour the honey mixture over the top and toss well to coat.
3 Roast for 30–40 minutes until brown and tender, occasionally spooning the released juices over the potatoes to baste. Serve hot.

SERVES 4

PREPARATION + COOKING
10 + 40 minutes

STORAGE
Leftovers will keep in the fridge for up to 2 days.

SERVE THIS WITH...
Apricot Turkey Burgers
(see page 107)
mixed salad
Summer Berry Crisp
(see page 134)

HEALTH BENEFITS
Orange-fleshed sweet potatoes are full of antioxidants, particularly beta-carotene and vitamin C, which help protect the body against the effects of ageing. They are also a good source of vitamin E, vital for a healthy heart and skin. Their high fibre content can help lower cholesterol and aid digestive health.

SERVES 4–6

PREPARATION + COOKING
10 + 30 minutes

STORAGE
Leftovers can be kept in the
fridge for up to 3 days.

SERVE THIS WITH...
Roasted Vegetables & Dukkah
  (see page 123)
fresh fruit and yogurt
Cranberry & Date Balls
  (see page 91)

HEALTH BENEFITS
New potatoes are a rich source
of vitamin C and B vitamins,
which are needed for energy
production. Most of their fibre,
vitamins and minerals are found
in the skin, so choose organic
potatoes, if possible, and leave
the skin on.

Ⓥ

lemon-paprika
new potatoes

This delicious recipe enhances the flavour
of roasted potatoes without the need for salt
or creamy dressings.

1kg/2lb 4oz baby new potatoes,
  scrubbed
3 tbsp olive oil
juice and grated zest of 1 lemon

1 tsp cumin seeds, lightly
  ground
1 tsp smoked paprika
freshly ground black pepper

1 Preheat the oven to 200°C/400°F/Gas 6. Cook the
potatoes in boiling water for 5 minutes until they start
to turn tender. Drain well, then transfer to a baking sheet.
2 Put the oil, lemon juice and zest, cumin and paprika in
a small bowl. Season to taste with black pepper and whisk
well. Pour the mixture over the potatoes and toss to coat.
3 Roast for 20–25 minutes, occasionally spooning the
released juices over the potatoes to baste. Serve hot or cold.

Ⓥ ⊘

coconut rice

This creamy, lightly spiced rice is the perfect accompaniment to curries and Asian dishes. Warming and wonderfully satisfying, it is sure to become a favourite with the whole family.

2 tbsp olive oil
1 onion, finely chopped
2 garlic cloves, crushed
4 cardamom pods, crushed
250g/9oz/1¼ cups brown
   basmati rice, rinsed

300ml/10½fl oz/1¼ cups
   coconut milk
1 small handful coriander
   leaves, chopped

1 Heat the oil in a large pan and fry the onion and garlic over a medium heat for 2–3 minutes until softened. Add the cardamom pods and rice and stir to coat in the oil.
2 Pour in the coconut milk and 100ml/3½fl oz/scant ½ cup water. Bring to the boil, then reduce the heat and simmer gently for 20 minutes until all the liquid has been absorbed.
3 Sprinkle with the coriander leaves and serve.

SERVES 4

PREPARATION + COOKING
5 + 25 minutes

STORAGE
Leftovers will keep in the fridge for up to 2 days.

SERVE THIS WITH...
Chicken Tikka (see page 106)
Chilli & Sesame Broccoli
  (see page 70)
Spice-poached Pears
  (see page 135)

HEALTH BENEFITS
Brown basmati rice is an excellent source of cholesterol-lowering fibre, B vitamins and manganese, which can help stabilize blood sugar levels. It releases its sugars more slowly than white rice so will keep you feeling fuller for longer.

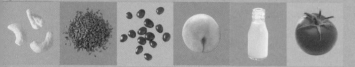

TEAS & SNACKS

One of the best ways to cut down on salt is to avoid processed foods, since the majority of salt we consume is 'hidden' in shop-bought products. Surprisingly, breads, cakes, biscuits, pastries and other sweet treats can be very high in salt. But make your own with these delicious, easy-to-follow recipes and you won't need to go without. Choose from a delectable selection of savoury options like Sun-dried Tomato Bread or Spicy Tortilla Chips, or satisfy a sweet tooth with a range of great-tasting treats such as Orange & Cranberry Muffins, Amaretto Biscotti or Mango & Coconut Tray Bake. These recipes are full of nutritious ingredients and bursting with natural flavours – so whatever you choose, you certainly won't feel deprived.

047

Ⓥ ⊘ ⊘ ⊘ ⊘

sesame crackers

These home-made crackers get their flavour from smoked paprika and sesame seeds, rather than from added salt.

MAKES 15–20

PREPARATION + COOKING
15 + 12 minutes

STORAGE
Keep in an airtight container for up to 4 days or freeze for up to 1 month.

SERVE THIS WITH…
Roasted Red Pepper Hummus (see page 42)
Sun-dried Tomato Dip (see page 43)
Orange & Cranberry Muffins (see page 86)
fresh fruit

HEALTH BENEFITS
Wholemeal flour is much higher in fibre and B vitamins than white refined versions. It also releases energy more slowly, keeping you feeling fuller for longer and helping to avoid energy slumps during the day.

125g/4½oz/scant 1 cup wholemeal flour
125g/4½oz/1 cup plain flour, plus extra for rolling
1 tsp baking powder
½ tsp smoked paprika
3 tbsp grated low-salt cheese, such as Emmental or Gruyère
4 tbsp sesame seeds
4 tbsp olive oil
scant 1 cup milk, plus extra for brushing

1 Preheat the oven to 190°C/375°F/Gas 5. Put the flours, baking powder, paprika, cheese and half the sesame seeds in a bowl. Add the oil and 4 tbsp of the milk and mix together with your hands. Gradually add more milk and continue mixing until the mixture forms a soft dough.
2 Tip the dough on to a lightly floured work surface. Roll it out to 2cm/¾in thick, then stamp out 15–20 rounds with an 8cm/3in pastry cutter. Put the rounds on a baking sheet, brush the tops with a little milk and sprinkle over the remaining sesame seeds.
3 Bake for 10–12 minutes until golden brown. Leave the crackers on the baking sheet for 1 minute, then transfer them to a wire rack to cool completely.

(V) (∅)

roasted spiced nuts

You can avoid the temptation to reach for a bag of salted nuts with this delicious, spicy, salt-free recipe. These nuts are simple to prepare but incredibly moreish. They are great as a snack on their own or sprinkled over salads to add extra crunch.

2 tbsp olive oil
225g/8oz/1½ cups unsalted mixed nuts, such as Brazil nuts, pecans, almonds, cashews and peanuts
¼ tsp garam masala
¼ tsp chilli powder

1 Heat the oil in a frying pan and add the nuts. Fry for 2–3 minutes, stirring occasionally, until they start to turn golden. You may have to do this in batches.
2 Transfer the nuts to a bowl, sprinkle the spices over the top and toss well to coat. Leave to cool before serving.

SERVES 4

PREPARATION + COOKING
5 + 6 minutes

STORAGE
Make in advance and keep in an airtight container in the fridge for up to 1 week.

SERVE THIS WITH...
Moroccan Burgers (see page 115)
wholemeal rolls
mixed salad

HEALTH BENEFITS
Nuts are a great energizing, protein rich food. Brazil nuts are exceptionally high in selenium, important for the immune system and healthy thyroid and sperm. They also contain plenty of heart-friendly omega-3 and omega-6 fatty acids, plus healthy monounsaturated fats.

Ⓥ Ⓞ ⓪ ⓖ

spicy tortilla chips

SERVES 4

PREPARATION + COOKING
5 + 10 minutes

STORAGE
Make in advance and keep in
an airtight container for up to
4 days.

SERVE THIS WITH...
Baked Eggs with Harissa
(see page 38)
Roasted Red Pepper Hummus
(see page 42)
Sun-dried Tomato Dip
(see page 43)

HEALTH BENEFITS
Wholemeal breads, rolls and
tortillas contain unrefined
complex carbohydrates, which
release their energy more slowly
than white, processed versions.
Choose reduced-salt varieties to
keep salt levels to a minimum.

A healthy alternative to traditional salty crisps,
these are simple to prepare and delicious
dipped into home-made salsas or dips. To make
these gluten-free, use 100 per cent corn tortillas.

1 egg white, lightly beaten   ½ tsp chilli powder
2 tbsp olive oil   ½ tsp cayenne pepper
1 tsp Dijon mustard   3 low-salt soft corn or
1 garlic clove, crushed   wholemeal tortillas

1 Preheat the oven to 180°C/350°F/Gas 4. Put the egg
white, oil, mustard, garlic, chilli powder and cayenne
pepper in a bowl and whisk well. Brush one side of each
tortilla with the egg mixture. Cut the tortillas into wedges
and put them, brushed-side up, on a baking sheet.
2 Bake for 5–10 minutes until crispy. Remove from the
oven, transfer to a wire rack and leave to cool.

Ⓥ ◐ ◈ ◈ ◐ ◐ ◈

pumpkin & seed bread

This quick recipe yields a light bread that is delicious served with soup or stews or lightly toasted for a healthy snack. Canned pumpkin purée is a great storecupboard ingredient that is also rich in immune-boosting antioxidants.

250g/9oz/1²/₃ cups wholemeal
    self-raising flour
1 tsp baking powder
a pinch chilli powder
55g/2oz/½ cup mixed seeds,
    such as sesame, sunflower
    and pumpkin

5 tbsp milk
2 tbsp honey
1 egg, lightly beaten
2 tbsp olive oil, plus extra
    for greasing
225g/8oz/1 cup canned
    pumpkin purée

1 Preheat the oven to 190°C/375°F/Gas 5. Put the flour, baking powder, chilli powder and half the seeds in a bowl and mix well. In a separate bowl, mix together the milk, honey, egg and oil, add this to the dry ingredients and stir with a wooden spoon until well mixed.
2 Tip the batter into a lightly greased 450g/1lb loaf tin, then sprinkle the remaining seeds over the top.
3 Bake for 30 minutes until golden brown and a skewer inserted into the centre of the loaf comes out clean. Leave to cool in the tin for 5 minutes, then transfer to a wire rack to cool completely before serving.

MAKES 1 x 450G/1LB LOAF

PREPARATION + COOKING
15 + 30 minutes

STORAGE
Make in advance, wrap and keep in the fridge for up to 3 days or freeze for up to 1 month.

SERVE THIS WITH...
Roasted Garlic & Tomato Soup
  (see page 45)
salads
Chocolate & Orange Soufflés
  (see page 133)

HEALTH BENEFITS
Pumpkins are a good source of carotenoids, which protect against cancer and heart disease. They also provide plenty of fibre, useful for lowering cholesterol and improving digestion.

Ⓥ Ⓐ Ⓕ Ⓐ Ⓐ Ⓑ

*sun-dried tomato bread

HEALTH BENEFITS
Tomatoes and olive oil are
a very healthy combination.
Carotenoids, abundant in
tomatoes, are fat-soluble, which
means they need to be eaten
with a little fat to be absorbed.
Olive oil is also a good source
of healthy monounsaturates,
useful for protecting against
heart disease.

This delicious Italian bread combines
sun-dried tomatoes and toasted nuts to
produce a wonderful rich flavour without the
need for any salt. The tomatoes not only add
a beautiful colour, they are also packed
full of carotenoids, important nutrients
for the skin and eyes that also offer
protection against certain cancers.
For a gluten-free version, use
a gluten-free flour mix.

500g/1lb 2oz/3⅓ cups strong
   wholemeal bread flour
7g/¼oz fast-acting dried yeast
55g/2oz/½ cup toasted nuts
8 sun-dried tomatoes in oil,
   drained and chopped

2 eggs
1 tbsp low-salt sun-dried
   tomato paste
4 tbsp olive oil, plus extra
   for greasing
1 tbsp honey

MAKES 1 x 900G/2LB LOAF

PREPARATION + COOKING
20 + 30 minutes + rising

STORAGE
Make in advance, wrap in
cling film or foil and keep in
an airtight container for up
to 3 days or freeze for up to
1 month.

SERVE THIS WITH...
Chicken & Artichoke Salad
 (see page 59)

1 Put the flour, yeast, nuts and tomatoes in a large bowl.
Stir, then make a well in the centre of the mixture.
2 In a separate bowl, mix together the eggs, tomato paste,
oil and honey. Pour the egg mixture into the well in the
flour and mix together, using your hands. Gradually add
275ml/9½fl oz/scant 1¼ cups warm water and continue
mixing until a soft dough forms. Knead in the bowl for
10 minutes until elastic, cover and leave to rise for 1 hour.
3 Knock back the dough, knead again for a few minutes
and shape into a large round loaf. Put the loaf on a lightly
oiled baking sheet, cover and leave to rise for 20 minutes.
Preheat the oven to 220°C/425°F/Gas 7.
4 Bake for 30 minutes until golden, then transfer to a wire
rack to cool completely before serving.

Toasting nuts is
a great way to enhance
their natural, sweet
flavour, so there's no
need for salt or other
additives.

MAKES 10

PREPARATION + COOKING
25 + 20 minutes + rising

STORAGE
Make in advance, wrap and keep in an airtight container for up to 3 days or freeze for up to 1 month. Warm through in the oven from frozen.

SERVE THIS WITH…
Vegetable Tagine with Dates & Almonds (see page 124)
Rosewater Rice Pudding with Strawberries (see page 128)

HEALTH BENEFITS
Many Indian spices are known for their healing properties. Cumin is a useful digestive aid and helps the body absorb nutrients. It can also stimulate the immune system and have an anti-mucosal effect, helping to clear coughs and colds.

Ⓥ Ⓕ Ⓖ ⓝ Ⓥ

spiced flatbreads

Completely salt-free, yet full of flavour, these Indian flatbreads are perfect for dipping into tagines and curries.

21g/¾oz sachets fast-acting
    dried yeast
2 tbsp honey
1 tbsp cumin seeds,
    dry-roasted and ground
1 tbsp coriander seeds,
    dry-roasted and ground

1 tbsp sesame seeds
500g/1lb 2oz/4 cups strong
    white bread flour
500g/1lb 2oz/3½ cups strong
    wholemeal bread flour
olive oil, for greasing

1 Put the yeast, honey and 310ml/10¾fl oz/1¼ cups lukewarm water in a bowl and stir until the yeast is dissolved. Set aside for 15 minutes.

2 Put the ground spices, sesame seeds and flours in a large bowl. Add the yeast mixture and an additional 310ml/10¾fl oz/1¼ cups lukewarm water and mix, using your hands, until the mixture forms a soft dough. Knead briefly, then cover the bowl and leave to rise for 1 hour.

3 Preheat the oven to 220°C/425°F/Gas 7. Divide the dough into 10 equal pieces and roll each one into a thin oval. Put them on lightly greased baking sheets and bake for 5–10 minutes until puffed up and golden. Transfer to a wire rack and leave to cool completely before serving.

Ⓥ Ⓞ ◉ ◉ ◉

chilli corn muffins

Cornmeal is high in B vitamins, which can help the body to cope with stress.

260g/9oz/2¼ cups cornmeal
100g/3½oz/heaped ¾ cup plain
flour
2 tsp baking powder
½ tsp chilli powder

125g/4½oz can sweetcorn, no
added salt or sugar, drained
2 eggs, beaten
125ml/4fl oz/½ cup olive oil,
plus extra for greasing
150ml/5fl oz/⅔ cup milk

1 Preheat the oven to 190°C/375°F/Gas 5. Put the corn-meal, flour, baking powder, chilli powder and sweetcorn in a bowl. In another bowl, mix together the eggs, oil and milk. Pour this mixture into the flour and stir briefly until a batter forms.
2 Divide the mixture into six or eight holes of a lightly greased muffin tin. Bake for 20–30 minutes until golden and firm to the touch. Leave the muffins to cool in the tin for 1 minute, then transfer to a wire rack and leave to cool completely before serving.

MAKES 6–8 MUFFINS

PREPARATION + COOKING
15 + 30 minutes

STORAGE
Make in advance and keep
in an airtight container for
up to 3 days or freeze for up
to 1 month.

SERVE THIS WITH...
Roasted Garlic & Tomato Soup
 (see page 45)
mixed salad
Baked Pear & Spice Puddings
 (see page 129)

HEALTH BENEFITS
Cornmeal is a rich source
of energy-giving carbohydrates,
fibre, potassium and B vitamins
– useful for balancing blood
sugar levels and great for
appetite control.

Ⓥ Ⓖ Ⓔ Ⓐ Ⓑ

fruit & seed tea bread

This delicious, fat-free tea bread is bursting with omega-rich seeds, warming spices and dried fruit. Soya flour and soya milk provide a heap of health-boosting phyto-oestrogens.

MAKES 1 x 900G/2LB LOAF

PREPARATION + COOKING
15 + 70 minutes + soaking

STORAGE
Make in advance, wrap in foil and keep in the fridge for up to 4 days or freeze for up to 1 month.

SERVE THIS WITH...
Cranberry & Cherry Compote (see page 25)
Asparagus & Herb Frittata (see page 54)
mixed salad
fresh fruit

HEALTH BENEFITS
Pumpkin seeds contain both omega-3 and omega-6 fatty acids and plenty of micro-nutrients like vitamin E and zinc, important for the immune system and healthy, glowing skin. They also contain calcium and magnesium, which are needed for strong bones and to relax muscles and blood vessels.

125g/4½oz/heaped 1 cup soya flour
125g/4½oz/scant 1 cup self-raising wholemeal flour
2 tsp baking powder
1 piece stem ginger, chopped
1 tsp ground cinnamon

200g/7oz/scant 1²/₃ cups mixed seeds, such as pumpkin, sunflower and flaxseed
115g/4oz/scant 1 cup raisins
100g/3½oz/²/₃ cup mixed dried berries
500ml/17fl oz/2 cups soya milk
4 tbsp honey
100ml/3½fl oz/scant ½ cup apple purée

1 Put the flours, baking powder, ginger, cinnamon, seeds and dried fruit in a large bowl. Put the soya milk, honey and apple purée in a saucepan and heat over a low heat until warm. Stir into the flour mixture and leave to stand for 30 minutes. Preheat the oven to 170°C/325°F/Gas 3.
2 Spoon the mixture into a lightly greased 900g/2lb loaf tin. Bake for 60–70 minutes until golden brown, risen and a skewer inserted into the centre of the loaf comes out clean. Leave to cool completely in the tin before turning out and serving.

apple crunch cake

This delicious cake, full of slow-releasing energy from the oats, wholemeal flour and apples, will keep hunger pangs away.

500g/1lb 2oz apples, peeled, cored and sliced
175g/6oz/scant 1¼ cups wholemeal self-raising flour
100g/3½oz/1 cup rolled oats
200g/7oz/scant 2 cups muesli, no added salt or sugar
1 tsp ground ginger
3 tbsp honey
4 tbsp olive oil
150ml/5fl oz/²/₃ cup natural yogurt

SERVES 8

PREPARATION + COOKING
15 + 55 minutes

STORAGE
Make in advance and keep in the fridge for up to 2 days.

SERVE THIS WITH…
Pan-fried Salmon with Tomato & Bean Salad (see page 56)
mixed salad
fresh fruit

HEALTH BENEFITS
Quercetin, an antioxidant found in many fruit and vegetables, including apples, helps protect cholesterol from oxidation and accumulating in the arteries. It is also known for its anti-inflammatory properties, making it useful for conditions such as arthritis, asthma and allergies.

1 Preheat the oven to 190°C/375°F/Gas 5. Put the apples in a saucepan with 3 tbsp water, cover and simmer over a medium heat for 5 minutes until soft. Transfer to a blender and blend for 1–2 minutes until smooth.

2 Put the flour, oats, muesli and ginger in a bowl, then mix in the honey, oil and yogurt.

3 Press half the oat mixture into a lightly greased 20cm/8in loose-bottom cake tin. Bake in the oven for 15 minutes until golden. Remove from the oven, spoon the apple purée over the top and sprinkle with the remaining oat mixture, then return to the oven and bake for a further 30–35 minutes until golden.

4 Leave to cool. Slice and serve at room temperature.

orange & cranberry muffins

HEALTH BENEFITS
All berries are packed full of antioxidants, particularly anthocyanins, as well as vitamin C to keep the immune system healthy. Cranberries and blueberries contain natural antibacterial properties that can help prevent and treat urinary tract infections such as cystitis.

These muffins make a great high-fibre treat without the added salt found in shop-bought varieties. Oat bran and flaxseeds are rich in soluble fibre, which can help regulate blood sugar levels and maintain a healthy bowel. Flaxseeds are an excellent source of essential fatty acids.

115g/4oz/scant 1 cup plain flour
90g/3¼oz/½ cup oat bran
55g/2oz/scant ½ cup ground
    flaxseed
2 tsp baking powder
1 orange, peeled and sliced,
    pips removed
55g/2oz/½ cup fructose

115ml/4fl oz/scant ½ cup
    buttermilk or natural yogurt
4 tbsp olive oil, plus extra
    for greasing
1 egg, beaten
55g/2oz/⅓ cup dried
    cranberries

MAKES 12

PREPARATION + COOKING
15 + 20 minutes

STORAGE
Make in advance and keep in an
airtight container in the fridge for
up to 4 days or freeze for up to
1 month.

SERVE THIS WITH...
Apricot Turkey Burgers
    (see page 107)
fresh fruit

1 Preheat the oven to 180°C/350°F/Gas 4. Put the flour,
oat bran, flaxseed and baking powder in a bowl and
mix together.
2 Put the orange, fructose, buttermilk, oil and egg in a
blender and blend until smooth. Pour this mixture into the
dry ingredients, add the cranberries and stir briefly.
3 Divide the mixture into twelve holes of a lightly greased
muffin tin. Bake for 20 minutes until golden brown and
firm to the touch. Leave the muffins to cool in the tin for
1 minute, then transfer to a wire rack. Serve warm or at
room temperature.

Oranges are a
great source of
vitamin C and contain
beta-sitosterol, a
plant sterol shown to
lower cholesterol.

057

V

mango & coconut tray bake

This salt-free slice, packed with the natural flavours of mango and coconut, is a nutritious, tropical snack the kids will love.

MAKES 16

PREPARATION + COOKING
10 + 35 minutes + soaking

STORAGE
Make in advance and keep in an airtight container in the fridge for up to 4 days or freeze for up to 1 month.

SERVE THIS WITH...
Seared Beef & Spinach Salad (see page 60)
egg or rice noodles
fresh fruit

HEALTH BENEFITS
Dried exotic fruit like mango and papaya make the perfect healthy snack. They are a rich source of potassium, important for balancing body fluids and lowering blood pressure.

125g/4½oz dried mango slices, without sugar, chopped
2 mangos, peeled, stoned and sliced
juice and grated zest of 3 limes
150ml/5fl oz/²/₃ cup olive oil
55g/2oz/½ cup rolled oats
150g/5½oz/scant 1¼ cups self-raising flour
150g/5½oz/scant 1¼ cups self-raising wholemeal flour
1 tsp baking powder
115g/4oz/1 cup desiccated coconut

1 Preheat the oven to 180°C/350°F/Gas 4. Put the dried mango in a heatproof bowl and cover with boiling water. Leave to soak for 30 minutes, then drain.
2 Put the fresh mango, lime juice and zest and oil in a blender and blend for 1–2 minutes until smooth.
3 Put the oats, flours, baking powder, coconut and dried mango in a bowl. Mix well, then stir in the mango purée.
4 Spoon the mixture into a lightly greased 25 x 30cm/ 10 x 12in baking tin and level the surface with a spatula. Bake for 30–35 minutes until golden brown. Leave to cool in the tin, then cut into 16 slices and serve.

Ⓥ ⊘ ⊘ ⊘ ⊘ ⊘

date & lemon oat bars

Cereal bars can often be high in salt, so this tangy, home-made slice is a great alternative.

Juice and grated zest of
  4 lemons
6 tbsp apple juice
325g/11½oz/2 cups dried pitted
  dates, chopped
5 tbsp honey
150ml/5fl oz/⅔ cup olive oil,
  plus extra for greasing

150g/5½oz/1½ cups rolled oats
175g/6oz/scant 1½ cups self-
  raising wholemeal flour
4 tbsp sunflower seeds
½ tsp bicarbonate of soda
115g/4oz/scant 1 cup ground
  almonds

1 Preheat the oven to 180°C/350°F/Gas 4. Put the lemon juice and zest, apple juice and 225g/8oz/1⅓ cups of the dates in a saucepan. Simmer over a medium heat for 1–2 minutes, then set aside to cool. Pour the mixture into a blender, add the honey and oil and blend until smooth.
2 Put all the remaining ingredients in a bowl, then stir in the date purée. Press the mixture into a lightly greased 25 x 30cm/10 x 12in baking tin. Bake for 25–30 minutes until golden and leave to cool. Cut into 16 bars and serve.

MAKES 16

PREPARATION + COOKING
15 + 35 minutes

STORAGE
Make in advance and keep in an airtight container in the fridge for up to 5 days or freeze for up to 1 month.

SERVE THIS WITH...
Lamb Koftas with Mint Yogurt
  (see page 114)
Citrus, Bean Sprout & Avocado
  Salad (see page 63)
fresh fruit

HEALTH BENEFITS
Full of natural sugars and iron, dates make a good choice for flagging energy levels. They also provide plenty of potassium, which can help regulate blood pressure. Using wholemeal flour and oats slows down the rate at which the sugars are released into the bloodstream, keeping you feeling fuller for longer.

059

Ⓥ Ⓞ ⊘ ⊘ ⊗ ⊛

amaretto biscotti

These crisp almond and apricot biscuits laced with amaretto are a healthy yet indulgent treat. Serve them with coffee at the end of a meal or with sorbets and ice creams.

MAKES 16

PREPARATION + COOKING
15 + 45 minutes

STORAGE
Make in advance and keep in an airtight container for up to 1 week.

SERVE THIS WITH...
Seared Salmon with Gremolata (see page 100)
Sun-dried Tomato Bread (see page 80)
mixed salad
Pomegranate-Orange Sorbet (see page 136)

HEALTH BENEFITS
Dried apricots are rich in lycopene and beta-carotene, important for a healthy heart, skin and eyes. They also provide plenty of iron, which can help prevent anaemia. Avoid bright orange dried apricots as they have been treated with sulphur.

100g/3½oz/scant 1 cup plain flour
1 tsp baking powder
75g/3oz/⅓ cup fructose
75g/3oz/scant ½ cup dried apricots, chopped

55g/2oz/⅓ cup blanched almonds, chopped
1 egg, beaten
1 tbsp amaretto liqueur
olive oil, for greasing

1 Preheat the oven to 180°C/350°F/Gas 4. Line a baking sheet with baking parchment.

2 Put the flour, baking powder, fructose, apricots and almonds in a bowl. Add the egg and amaretto and stir until the mixture forms a soft dough.

3 Roll the mixture into a long log about 5cm/2in wide and place on a lightly greased baking sheet. Bake for 25 minutes until golden.

4 Remove from the oven but leave the oven on. Leave the log to cool for 10 minutes, then cut it at an angle into 0.5cm/¼in slices. Arrange the slices on the baking sheet and bake for 8–10 minutes on each side until crisp. Transfer to a wire rack to cool, then serve.

Ⓥ ⏀ ✦

cranberry & date balls

Rather than snacking on sweets and chocolate, which can contain added salt, choose these delicious, energy-boosting morsels when you fancy a treat.

125g/4½oz/¾ cup dried
   cranberries
55g/2oz/⅓ cup dried pitted
   dates

1 tbsp apple juice
2–3 tbsp ground almonds
55g/2oz/½ cup desiccated
   coconut

1 Put the cranberries, dates and apple juice in a food processor and blend until smooth. Add enough of the ground almonds to form a stiff paste.
2 Shape teaspoons of the mixture into 10–12 balls of equal size and roll them in the coconut to coat. Chill until required, then serve.

MAKES 10–12

PREPARATION
15 minutes

STORAGE
Make in advance and keep in the fridge for up to 1 week.

SERVE THIS WITH...
Pesto Tuna Wraps (see page 48) fresh fruit and yogurt

HEALTH BENEFITS
Dried fruit contains plenty of antioxidants, B vitamins and iron, and, since it is naturally sweet, there is no need to add extra sugar. Rich in potassium, it can help to lower blood pressure and reduce fluid retention.

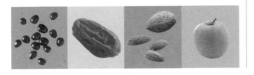

DINNERS

Takeaways and ready meals can be tempting at the end of a long day, but they often contain more salt than your whole day's recommended amount, not to mention excess calories and fat. Creating a delicious, satisfying evening meal that is also low in salt doesn't need to be a struggle or take hours to prepare. This chapter is packed with mouthwatering main courses, such as Apricot Turkey Burgers and Pesto-crusted Chicken, which are sure to be a hit with the kids. There are plenty of speedy weekday dishes, such as Baked Sesame Trout; vegetarian delights, like Sweet Potato & Coconut Curry; and more indulgent meals, such as Roasted Quail with Pomegranate Molasses. These fabulous, low-salt dishes will delight your family and friends.

061

SERVES 4

PREPARATION + COOKING
10 + 10 minutes

STORAGE
Best eaten on the day they
are made.

SERVE THIS WITH…
Citrus, Bean Sprout & Avocado
  Salad (see page 63)
Apple Crunch Cake (see page 85)
fresh fruit

HEALTH BENEFITS
Many herbs have healing
properties and contain a
wealth of minerals. Basil is rich
in flavonoids and volatile oils,
which have antibacterial and
anti-inflammatory properties.
It also contains magnesium
and potassium to help relax
muscles and blood vessels and
regulate blood pressure.

scallops en papillote

Cooking seafood in parchment or foil bags
helps retain all the flavour and nutrients.

1 tbsp olive oil, plus extra
    for brushing
2 tbsp mirin
2 tbsp chopped basil

2 tbsp lemon juice
1 tsp grated lemon zest
16 large scallops, cleaned
    and trimmed

1 Preheat the oven to 200°C/400°F/Gas 6. Cut out four
35cm/14in squares of foil or baking parchment and brush
each one lightly with oil.
2 Put the oil, mirin, basil, lemon juice and zest in a bowl
and mix well.
3 Put 4 scallops in the middle of each piece of foil. Drizzle
the dressing over the top and gather up the foil to form a
parcel. Put the parcels on a baking sheet and bake for 10
minutes until the scallops are cooked. Open the parcels
and serve.

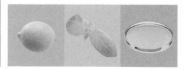

spaghetti with chilli mussels

The Thai seasonings in this pasta dish burst with flavour. Mussels are the perfect low-fat fast food, containing plenty of heart-protecting folate and B vitamins, as well as immune-boosting iron and zinc.

2 tbsp olive oil
3 garlic cloves, crushed
2 tsp grated root ginger
2 red chillies, deseeded and
    finely chopped
12 cherry tomatoes, halved

900g/2lb mussels in their
    shells, cleaned
125ml/4fl oz/½ cup dry white
    wine
350g/12oz spaghetti
1 handful basil, chopped

1 Heat the oil in a frying pan over a medium heat. Add the garlic, ginger and chillies and cook for 1 minute. Add the tomatoes, mussels and wine, then cover with a lid and steam for 3–4 minutes, shaking the pan, until the mussels open. Discard any that don't open.
2 Cook the spaghetti in a large pan of boiling water for about 8 minutes, or according to the packet instructions, until al dente. Drain well and add it to the mussels. Toss gently to mix, sprinkle with the basil and serve.

SERVES 4

PREPARATION + COOKING
15 + 15 minutes

STORAGE
Best eaten immediately, but leftovers will keep in the fridge until the following day.

SERVE THIS WITH...
Summer Leaves with Mango
  Vinaigrette (see page 66)
Tropical Fruit Skewers
  (see page 139)

HEALTH BENEFITS
Ginger and chillies are wonderful circulation boosters and can help detoxify the body. Ginger also contains aromatic oils that have potent antiseptic properties and can help prevent nausea. Garlic is a powerful antioxidant, with volatile oils that can boost heart health and immune function.

seafood stir-fry

This version of a favourite Chinese takeaway
is also great with chicken, fish or vegetables.

600g/1lb 5oz prepared seafood,
   such as prawns, scallops
   and squid rings
4 spring onions, chopped
1 red pepper, deseeded and
   sliced
1 garlic clove, crushed
225g/8oz canned pineapple
   pieces in juice, drained and
   juice reserved
1 tbsp olive oil

Sweet & Sour Sauce:
2 tsp cornflour
2 tbsp rice vinegar
1cm/½in piece root ginger,
   peeled and grated
1 tbsp soft brown sugar
2 tbsp tomato ketchup,
   no added salt or sugar
1 tbsp tamari

1 Put the seafood, spring onions, pepper and garlic
in a bowl and mix well.
2 To make the sauce, blend together the cornflour
and vinegar. Put in a saucepan with the ginger, sugar,
ketchup, tamari and pineapple juice, bring to the boil
and then reduce the heat. Simmer over a low heat for
5 minutes until thickened.
3 Heat the oil in a wok. Add the seafood and vegetables
and stir-fry for 3–4 minutes until cooked. Add the
pineapple pieces and sauce to the wok and cook, stirring,
for 1–2 minutes until heated through, then serve.

thai crab cakes

Many ready-made fish cakes contain salt for flavouring and as a preservative. Using lime and wasabi paste (a fiery Japanese horse-radish) in these crab cakes makes them naturally flavourful without added salt.

300g/10½oz white crab meat
2 spring onions, finely chopped
1 tsp wasabi paste
1 tsp tamari
¼ tsp chilli powder

1 handful coriander leaves, chopped
2 tsp lime juice
2 tbsp gluten-free flour
1 tbsp olive oil

1 Put all the ingredients, except the oil, in a food processor and blend until the mixture forms a coarse paste. Put the paste in a bowl, cover and chill for 15 minutes.
2 Using your hands, shape the mixture into 8 patties of equal size. Heat the oil in a frying pan until hot. Fry the crab cakes for 3–4 minutes on each side until golden brown and cooked through. Serve hot.

SERVES 4

PREPARATION + COOKING
15 + 15 minutes + chilling

STORAGE
Make in advance and keep, uncooked, in the fridge for up to 2 days or freeze for up to 1 month

SERVE THIS WITH...
Asian Coleslaw (see page 67)
Garlic & Chilli Sauce
  (see page 51)
Spice-poached Pears
  (see page 135)

HEALTH BENEFITS
Crab is an excellent source of protein and of many heart-protecting vitamins, including folate and vitamin B6, and the minerals selenium, magnesium, potassium and zinc. It also contains omega-3 fatty acids.

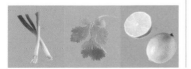

065

steamed snapper

Steaming is one of the best ways of retaining all the flavour and nutrients in food, especially for delicate fish.

SERVES 4

PREPARATION + COOKING
10 + 15 minutes

STORAGE
Marinate the fish in advance and keep in the fridge for up to 1 day.

SERVE THIS WITH...
Coconut Rice (see page 73)
Asian Coleslaw (see page 67)
Baked Pear & Spice Puddings
   (see page 129)

HEALTH BENEFITS
Citrus fruit contains a wealth of plant chemicals and antioxidant flavonoids that promote a healthy immune system, reduce inflammation, fight cancer and help prevent cardiovascular disease. It is also rich in fibre, making it excellent for the digestive system.

2 red snapper, about 500g/
   1lb 2oz each, cleaned
   and scaled
juice and grated zest of
   1 lemon
juice and grated zest of
   1 orange

2cm/¾in piece root ginger,
   peeled and grated
1 small red chilli, deseeded
   and chopped
2 spring onions, chopped
1 handful coriander leaves

1 Using a sharp knife, cut 5–6 diagonal slashes on each side of the fish. Put them on a heatproof plate that will fit into a steamer or put each one on a large square of foil.
2 Put the lemon and orange juice and zest, ginger, chilli, spring onions and coriander in a bowl and mix well. Pour this over the fish. Seal the foil parcels, if using.
3 Steam for 15 minutes until the fish is cooked. Transfer the fish to plates, drizzle over the cooking juices and serve.

thai fish balls in coconut

The fragrant herbs and spices in this dish provide loads of flavour without added salt.

650g/1lb 7oz firm white fish
    fillets, such as coley, cod
    or haddock
2 garlic cloves, crushed
2 tbsp cornflour
1 handful coriander leaves,
    chopped
1 tsp lemon juice

Coconut Sauce:
2 shallots, chopped
2 red chillies, deseeded and
    chopped
2 garlic cloves
1 tbsp olive oil
3 tomatoes, deseeded and
    chopped
400ml/14fl oz canned coconut
    milk

1 Put the fish, garlic, cornflour, coriander and lemon juice in a food processor and blend for 2–3 minutes until the mixture forms a paste. Shape the mixture into 8 balls.
2 Put the shallots, chillies and garlic in a food processor and blend until the mixture forms a paste. Heat the oil in a large frying pan, add the paste and cook for 1 minute.
3 Add the tomatoes, coconut milk and fish balls. Bring to the boil, then reduce the heat and simmer for 5–7 minutes, turning occasionally, until the fish is cooked through and the sauce has thickened. Serve immediately.

SERVES 4

PREPARATION + COOKING
5 + 8 minutes

STORAGE
Make in advance and keep, uncooked, in the fridge for up to 1 day or freeze for up to 1 month.

SERVE THIS WITH...
Spiced Flatbreads (see page 82)
Chilli & Sesame Broccoli
    (see page 70)
Pomegranate-Orange Sorbet
    (see page 136)

HEALTH BENEFITS
White fish, such as coley, is a great source of protein and is also low in fat. The garlic, chillies and shallots are potent immune boosters and fantastic foods for the heart – reducing 'bad' cholesterol and high blood pressure and making the blood less sticky.

067

Salmon contains a chemical called dimethylaminoethanol, or DMAE, an antioxidant that stimulates nerve function and protects cells from free radical damage. It is also an excellent source of omega-3 fats, renowned for reducing the risk of heart disease and supporting the cardiovascular system.

*seared salmon with gremolata

Gremolata, an Italian mixture of parsley, lemon zest and garlic, has a punchy flavour without adding salt. Quick to make and full of vital immune-boosting antioxidants, it can also be stirred into pasta and rice dishes or drizzled over seared beef or lamb. The salmon in this recipe is an excellent source of omega-3 fats.

1 large handful flat-leaf
   parsley, finely chopped
juice and grated zest of
   1 lemon
2 garlic cloves, crushed
3 tbsp olive oil

4 salmon fillets, skin on
10 red cherry tomatoes, halved
10 yellow cherry tomatoes,
   halved
freshly ground black pepper

SERVES 4

PREPARATION + COOKING
10 + 8 minutes

STORAGE
Prepare the gremolata in
advance and keep in the fridge
for up to 3 days.

SERVE THIS WITH...
steamed green beans
or watercress salad
Lemon-Berry Cheesecake
   (see page 130)

1 Put the parsley, lemon juice and zest, garlic and 2 tbsp of the oil in a bowl. Mix well.

2 Pour the remaining 1 tbsp oil over the salmon fillets and season with black pepper. Heat a frying pan until hot. Sear the salmon, skin-side down, for 2–3 minutes until golden. Turn the salmon over and cook for a further 4–5 minutes until cooked through.

3 Put the tomatoes in a bowl, add about 1 tbsp of the gremolata and toss well to coat. Spoon the tomatoes on to four serving plates and top with the salmon. Drizzle the remaining gremolata over the salmon and serve.

The anti-
inflammatory
components in parsley
and basil can ease
arthritis and bowel
inflammation.

grilled sesame trout

This speedy, nutrient-rich meal contains a wealth of health-promoting vitamins, minerals and essential fatty acids. The sesame seeds add a wonderful crunchy texture to the dish and contain a compound called sesamin that helps protect the heart and liver.

SERVES 4

PREPARATION + COOKING
5 + 8 minutes

STORAGE
Prepare the fish in advance and keep in the fridge overnight until ready to cook.

SERVE THIS WITH…
Mint & Lemon Courgettes
  (see page 69)
Orange-Honey Sweet Potatoes
  (see page 71)
Cherry & Ricotta Tarts
  (see page 132)

HEALTH BENEFITS
Trout is rich in omega-3 fatty acids, important for healthy skin, joints and heart. Sesame oil and seeds are high in omega-6 fatty acids and vitamin E for healthy skin and circulation, plus B vitamins to help the body cope with stress.

4 trout fillets, about 200g/7oz
   each, skin on
4½ tsp sesame oil

4 tbsp sesame seeds
freshly ground black pepper

1 Preheat the grill to high. Brush the trout with about half the sesame oil and season with black pepper. Press the seeds onto the top and sides of the fillets.
2 Heat a frying pan over a high heat, then add the trout, skin-side down, and cook for 3–4 minutes until the skin is crisp.
3 Transfer the trout, skin-side down, to a baking sheet and drizzle with the remaining oil. Grill for 3–4 minutes, until golden and cooked, then serve.

griddled tuna with mango & wasabi salsa

Wasabi, Japanese horseradish, is a great way to add vibrant flavour without adding salt.

5 tbsp olive oil
juice of 1 lime
1 garlic clove, crushed
4 tuna steaks, about 2cm/¾in
   thick

Mango & Wasabi Salsa:
2 tbsp lime juice
¼ tsp wasabi paste
1 mango, peeled, stoned and
   chopped
2 spring onions, chopped
1 tomato, deseeded and finely
   chopped
1 handful coriander leaves,
   chopped

1 Put the oil, lime juice and garlic in a bowl. Mix well, add the tuna steaks and leave to marinate for 30 minutes.
2 To make the salsa, put the lime juice and wasabi in a bowl, mix until blended and then stir in the remaining ingredients. Set aside.
3 Heat a griddle pan until hot, add the tuna steaks and cook for 2–3 minutes on each side until cooked. Serve with the salsa.

SERVES 4

PREPARATION + COOKING
15 + 6 minutes + marinating

STORAGE
Leftover tuna steaks can be kept in the fridge for up to 2 days. Serve them cold in pitta breads or add them to salads.

SERVE THIS WITH...
Asian Coleslaw (see page 67)
Spiced Flatbreads (see page 82)
Pomegranate-Orange Sorbet
  (see page 136)

HEALTH BENEFITS
Fresh tuna is an excellent source of omega-3 fats known as DHA (docosahexaenoic acid) and EPA (eicosapentaenoic acid). They are vital for brain function and a healthy nervous system and can boost our mood. Fresh tuna is a better choice than canned as the canning process destroys the omega-3 fats.

070

SERVES 4

PREPARATION + COOKING
10 + 25 minutes + marinating

STORAGE
Marinate the chicken in the
fridge the night before to allow
the flavours to develop.

SERVE THIS WITH...
Fruity Quinoa Salad
  (see page 62)
green salad
Rosewater Rice Pudding with
  Strawberries (see page 128)

HEALTH BENEFITS
Spices, such as cumin, chilli
and coriander, are great digestive
aids and are a traditional Asian
remedy for gastro-intestinal
disorders. They also possess
antimicrobial and antibacterial
properties, useful for fighting
coughs and colds.

chermoula-spiced chicken

The spicy marinade known as chermoula uses
herbs and spices, rather than salt, for flavour.

1 tsp ground cumin
1 tsp ground coriander
1 handful coriander leaves,
  chopped
1 handful parsley, chopped
1 red chilli, deseeded and
  chopped

1 garlic clove, crushed
juice and grated zest of
  1 lemon
½ tsp paprika
4 chicken breast fillets
1 tbsp olive oil

1 Put all the ingredients, except the chicken and oil, in
a bowl and mix well. Rub the mixture all over the chicken
fillets. Cover and chill for 2–3 hours or overnight.
2 Preheat the oven to 180°C/350°F/Gas 4. Put the chicken
in a roasting tin, drizzle with the oil and bake for 20–25
minutes or until cooked through and the juices run clear.
Serve immediately.

pesto-crusted chicken

Roasting the chicken with this delicious pesto keeps the meat moist and succulent. Chicken provides plenty of B vitamins, which are needed to make energy and respond to stress.

1 recipe quantity Pumpkin Seed
   Pesto (see page 48)
4 chicken breasts, skin on

1 tbsp olive oil
juice of 1 lemon

1 Preheat the oven to 200°C/400°F/Gas 6. Ease the skin away from the chicken, leaving it intact on one side. Spread the top of each breast with the pesto and pat the skin back over to seal.
2 Heat 1 tsp of the oil in a frying pan. Add the breasts, skin-side down, and sear for 1–2 minutes until golden.
3 Transfer the chicken to a roasting tin and drizzle with the lemon juice and remaining oil. Bake for 20–30 minutes until cooked through and the juices run clear, then serve.

SERVES 4

PREPARATION + COOKING
15 + 35 minutes

STORAGE
Keep leftover chicken in the fridge for up to 2 days.

SERVE THIS WITH...
Orange-Honey Sweet Potatoes
   (see page 71)
Balsamic-roasted Beetroot
   (see page 68)
mixed salad
Chocolate & Orange Soufflés
   (see page 133)

HEALTH BENEFITS
Olive oil is a rich source of monounsaturated fat, which has a protective role in preventing heart disease and helps maintain levels of 'good' cholesterol in the body. It is also less susceptible to damage from heat than sunflower and other seed oils.

PREPARATION + COOKING
15 + 10 minutes + marinating

STORAGE
Leftovers can be kept in the
fridge and used in wraps or pitta
breads the following day.

SERVE THIS WITH…
Coconut Rice (see page 73)
Asian Coleslaw (see page 67)
mixed salad
Pomegranate-Orange Sorbet
(see page 136)

HEALTH BENEFITS
Yogurt is not only a great
source of calcium for healthy
bones and teeth, it also contains
probiotic bacteria that may
help to boost immunity, protect
against infection and support the
digestive system. The calcium
content is similar in low-fat and
full-fat varieties.

chicken tikka

Home-made curry sauces and pastes don't
have to be complicated or time-consuming.

150ml/5fl oz/²/₃ cup low-fat
   Greek yogurt
½ onion, finely chopped
2.5cm/1in piece root ginger,
   peeled and grated
1 garlic clove, crushed
1 tsp ground coriander

2 tbsp lemon juice
½ tsp turmeric
1 tsp garam masala
4 skinless chicken breasts,
   cut into bite-sized pieces
olive oil, for greasing

1 Put all the ingredients, except the chicken and oil, in
a bowl and mix well. Add the chicken, cover and marinate
in the fridge for 2–3 hours.
2 Soak eight bamboo skewers in water for 30 minutes.
Preheat the grill to medium.
3 Thread the chicken on to the skewers and put them on
a greased baking sheet or grill rack. Grill for 7–9 minutes,
turning halfway through, until lightly charred, cooked
through and the juices run clear, then serve.

apricot turkey burgers

These turkey burgers have a subtle sweetness, thanks to the addition of dried apricots.

125g/4½oz/¾ cup dried
   apricots, finely chopped
2 tbsp orange juice
450g/1lb turkey breast mince

2 shallots, finely chopped
2 tbsp chopped parsley
2 tbsp olive oil, plus extra
   for greasing

1 Put the apricots and orange juice in a large bowl and leave to soak for 5 minutes.

2 Add the turkey, shallots and parsley to the apricots and mix well. Using wet hands, shape the mixture into 8 small patties or 4 large burgers. Cover and chill for 30 minutes.

3 Preheat the grill to high. Put the burgers on a lightly greased baking sheet, then brush them with the oil. Grill for 10 minutes on each side until cooked through. Alternatively, pan-fry the burgers for 3–4 minutes on each side. Serve hot.

SERVES 4

PREPARATION + COOKING
15 + 20 minutes + chilling

STORAGE
Make in advance and keep, uncooked, in the fridge for up to 2 days or freeze for up to 1 month.

SERVE THIS WITH...
wholemeal rolls
mixed salad
Orange-Honey Sweet Potatoes
  (see page 71)
Grilled Figs with Honey & Lemon
  Yogurt (see page 138)

HEALTH BENEFITS
Turkey is a nutritious, protein-rich food, low in saturated fat and incredibly high in tryptophan, which is converted by the body into serotonin – the 'feel-good hormone' that can help us sleep. Turkey is also a good source of the antioxidant selenium, important for a healthy immune system.

074

SERVES 4

PREPARATION + COOKING
15 + 30 minutes + marinating

STORAGE
Leftover quail will keep in
the fridge for up to 2 days.
Serve it cold with salad.

SERVE THIS WITH...
mixed salad
Fruity Quinoa Salad
  (see page 62)
Lemon-Berry Cheesecake
  (see page 130)

HEALTH BENEFITS
Poultry and game birds, such
as chicken, quail, turkey and
duck, are good sources of
stress-busting B vitamins, iron,
zinc and protein – important for
immune health, tissue repair and
building new cells. B vitamins,
especially folate, help lower
levels of homocysteine, a
high level of which is linked
to heart disease.

roasted quail with pomegranate molasses

Pomegranate molasses adds a delightful
sweet-sour taste to this dish.

4 oven-ready quail
1 pomegranate, halved

Marinade:
4 tbsp pomegranate molasses
2 garlic cloves, crushed
½ tsp ground cinnamon
1 tbsp olive oil

Dressing:
3 tbsp pomegranate molasses
juice and grated zest of
  ½ lemon
1 tsp honey
3 tbsp olive oil

1 Put all the marinade ingredients in a bowl and mix well.
Pour it over the quail, cover and chill for 1–2 hours.
2 Put all the dressing ingredients in a bowl and mix well.
3 Preheat the oven to 200°C/400°F/Gas 6. Put the quail in
a roasting tin and bake for 30 minutes, turning once, until
cooked through and the juices run clear. Remove from the
oven and leave to rest for 5 minutes.
4 Hold the pomegranate over a bowl and bash with a
wooden spoon to release the seeds. Slice the quail and
arrange on four serving plates. Drizzle the dressing over
the top, sprinkle with the pomegranate seeds and serve.

citrus seared duck

Fennel is rich in potassium, which can help regulate sodium levels in the body.

3 clementines
1 tbsp fish sauce
juice of 1 lime
4 duck breasts
1 tbsp olive oil

1 fennel bulb, finely chopped
1 red onion, chopped
2 garlic cloves, chopped
freshly ground black pepper

1 Preheat the oven to 200°C/400°F/Gas 6. Juice 2 of the clementines and divide the third into segments. Put the juice and segments in a bowl and mix in the fish sauce and lime juice.

2 Cut 5–6 diagonal slashes on the skin of the duck and season with black pepper. Heat a frying pan until hot. Sear the duck for 2–3 minutes on each side until golden, then reduce the heat and cook, skin-side down, for 10 minutes. Transfer to a roasting tin and bake for 10 minutes, or until cooked through and the juices run clear.

3 Heat the oil in the pan, add the fennel, onion and garlic and cook over a medium-low heat for 3–4 minutes until softened slightly. Add the clementine mixture and simmer for 1–2 minutes until the sauce is bubbling and syrupy.

4 Leave the duck to rest for 5 minutes, then slice it. Spoon the vegetables and sauce over the top and serve.

SERVES 4

PREPARATION + COOKING
15 + 35 minutes

STORAGE
Make the clementine mixture in step 1 in advance and keep it in the fridge for up to 3 hours. The cooked duck can be stored in the fridge for up to 2 days.

SERVE THIS WITH...
Orange-Honey Sweet Potatoes (see page 71)
mixed salad
Cherry & Ricotta Tarts (see page 132)

HEALTH BENEFITS
Although duck is high in cholesterol, it is actually low in saturated fat, especially if the skin is removed. It is a good source of iron for a healthy immune system and of stress-busting vitamin B2. The citrus sauce provides plenty of immune-boosting vitamin C.

SERVES 4

PREPARATION + COOKING
5 + 20 minutes

STORAGE
Leftovers will keep in the fridge until the following day.

SERVE THIS WITH...
mashed sweet potato
Balsamic-roasted Beetroot
  (see page 68)
fresh fruit
Amaretto Biscotti (see page 90)

HEALTH BENEFITS
Garlic is a heart-healthy food that helps to lower high blood pressure and cholesterol. It can also reduce the risk of heart attack and strokes by making the blood less sticky and less likely to clot.

marsala pork cutlets

Marsala, a fortified wine from Italy, has a sweet, robust flavour that makes it a perfect accompaniment to pork.

4 pork cutlets	1 tbsp butter
2 tbsp plain flour	2 garlic cloves, crushed
2 tbsp olive oil	6 tbsp Marsala
4 sage leaves	freshly ground black pepper

1 Dust the pork with the flour and season with black pepper. Heat the oil in a frying pan and add the sage leaves and pork. Cook the pork for 6–8 minutes on each side until cooked through. Remove the cutlets from the pan and keep them warm.

2 Add the butter, garlic and Marsala to the pan. Heat for 3–4 minutes until thickened.

3 Spoon the Marsala sauce over the pork and serve.

slow-roasted caribbean pork

Limes contain bioflavonoids, which, together with vitamin C, strengthen blood vessels and support the cardiovascular system.

1kg/2lb 4oz boned shoulder of pork, skin scored
1 red pepper, deseeded and cut into chunks
½ pineapple, cored and cut into wedges
1 red chilli, deseeded and chopped
1 red onion, chopped

1 large handful coriander leaves
juice and grated zest of 1 lime
1 garlic clove, chopped
200ml/7fl oz/generous ¾ cup coconut cream
¼ tsp ground cinnamon
2 tbsp olive oil

1 Preheat the oven to 180°C/350°F/Gas 4. Put the pork, pepper and pineapple in a large roasting tin. Put the remaining ingredients in a food processor and blend for 2–3 minutes until smooth. Pour the mixture over the pork. If time allows, cover and leave to marinate in the fridge for 1–2 hours or overnight.

2 Cover the tin with foil and roast for 2 hours, frequently spooning the juices over to baste. Remove from the oven and leave to rest for 15 minutes. Slice and serve with the vegetables and pan juices spooned over the pork.

SERVES 4

PREPARATION + COOKING
15 + 2 hours + marinating

STORAGE
Marinate the pork in advance and keep in the fridge overnight.

SERVE THIS WITH...
Lemon-Paprika New Potatoes (see page 72)
mixed salad
Tropical Fruit Skewers (see page 139)

HEALTH BENEFITS
Coconut is a rich source of lauric acid, which has antiviral and antibacterial properties to help the body fight infections. Coconut oil is very stable and is not damaged by heat, making it an excellent choice for cooking.

vietnamese pork noodles

This Asian version of spaghetti Bolognese is low in salt, easy to make and a hit with kids.

1 tbsp tamari
2 tbsp sweet chilli sauce
juice of 1 lime
1 tbsp sesame oil
2 spring onions, chopped

500g/1lb 2oz pork mince
250g/9oz rice noodles
½ cucumber, cut into
 matchsticks
4 tbsp natural yogurt

1 Put the tamari, sweet chilli sauce, lime juice and 5 tbsp water in a bowl and mix well.

2 Heat the oil in a wok. Add the onions and pork and cook over a medium heat for 3–4 minutes, stirring occasionally, until browned. Add the tamari mixture and simmer for 6–8 minutes until the meat is cooked.

3 Meanwhile, put the noodles in a heatproof bowl, cover with boiling water and leave to stand for about 4 minutes, or according to the packet instructions, until tender. Drain well, add the noodles to the wok and toss.

4 Divide the pork and noodles into four serving bowls. Mix together the cucumber and yogurt, spoon it over the noodles and serve immediately.

polenta-crusted lamb

Rather than coating the lamb in breadcrumbs, which can be high in salt, these cutlets have a lighter polenta crust that is flavoured with fresh herbs. The coating works equally well on fish and chicken. Make this recipe gluten-free by using gluten-free flour.

8 lamb cutlets
2 tbsp plain flour
1 egg, beaten
75g/2½oz/½ cup polenta

2 tsp finely chopped thyme
2 tsp finely chopped rosemary
2 garlic cloves, crushed

1 Preheat the grill to high. Flatten the lamb cutlets lightly with a rolling pin, then dust them with the flour.
2 Put the egg in a shallow bowl. Mix together the polenta, herbs and garlic and put the mixture on a plate. Dip the lamb in the egg, then coat with the polenta.
3 Put the cutlets on a baking sheet and grill for 5 minutes on each side until golden and cooked through, then serve.

SERVES 4

PREPARATION + COOKING
10 + 10 minutes

STORAGE
Make in advance and keep in the fridge for up to 1 day.

SERVE THIS WITH...
Lemon-Paprika New Potatoes
  (see page 72)
Mint & Lemon Courgettes
  (see page 69)
Summer Berry Crisp
  (see page 134)

HEALTH BENEFITS
Lamb, like other red meat, is a good source of iron and protein. It also provides plenty of B vitamins, especially B12, useful for boosting our mood as well as maintaining a healthy heart.

MAKES 10

PREPARATION + COOKING
20 + 12 minutes + chilling

STORAGE
Keep the uncooked koftas in the fridge for up to 2 days or freeze for up to 1 month.

SERVE THIS WITH...
Summer Leaves with Mango Vinaigrette (see page 66)
Spiced Flatbreads (see page 82)
Grilled Figs with Honey & Lemon Yogurt (see page 138)

HEALTH BENEFITS
Onions contain a substance called allicin, a natural antibiotic that helps fight off infections. Red onions are particularly rich in quercetin, an antioxidant that has anti-inflammatory properties and helps protect against cancer. Great for the heart too, onions are a useful diuretic, and they help regulate blood pressure and lower cholesterol.

lamb koftas with mint yogurt

These spicy koftas make wonderful finger food at barbecues.

900g/2lb lamb mince
2 onions, grated
2 garlic cloves, crushed
2 tsp ground coriander
2 tsp ground cumin
1 tsp chilli powder
2 tbsp chopped parsley
olive oil, for brushing

Mint & Yogurt Dressing:
150ml/5fl oz/²/₃ cup natural yogurt
2 tbsp chopped mint
freshly ground black pepper

1 Put the lamb, onion, garlic, spices and parsley in a large bowl. Mix well, cover and chill for 1 hour.
2 To make the dressing, put the yogurt and mint in a bowl, mix well and season to taste with black pepper. Cover and chill until ready to serve.
3 Soak ten bamboo skewers in water for 30 minutes. Preheat a barbecue or grill to high.
4 Divide the lamb mixture into 10 equal pieces. Press each piece around a skewer to make a long sausage-shaped kofta. Brush with oil, then barbecue or grill the koftas for 10–12 minutes, turning frequently, until golden brown and cooked through. Serve with the yogurt sauce.

moroccan burgers

Serve these delicious burgers with a home-made tomato sauce, rather than salty, sugary, shop-bought ketchup.

1 red chilli, deseeded and
   chopped
1 large bunch coriander
juice of ½ lemon
2 garlic cloves, crushed

1 tsp paprika
½ red onion, finely chopped
500g/1lb 2oz lean beef mince
olive oil, for greasing

1 Put the chilli, coriander, lemon juice, garlic and paprika in a food processor and blend for 1–2 minutes until the mixture forms a paste. Put the onion and mince in a large bowl, add the chilli paste and mix well, using your hands.
2 Shape the mixture into 8 burgers. Cover and chill for 30 minutes.
3 Preheat the grill to high. Put the burgers on a lightly greased baking sheet and grill for 7–8 minutes on each side until cooked through, then serve.

MAKES 8/SERVES 4

PREPARATION + COOKING
15 + 16 minutes + chilling

STORAGE
Prepare in advance and keep the uncooked burgers in the fridge for up to 2 days or freeze for up to 1 month.

SERVE THIS WITH...
Tomato Sauce (see page 19)
wholemeal rolls
lettuce and sliced tomato
Chocolate & Orange Soufflés
   (see page 133)
fresh fruit

HEALTH BENEFITS
Tomatoes are rich in carotenoids, which are important antioxidants that can help slow down the ageing process, reduce the risk of heart disease and stroke and help guard the skin and eyes from sun damage. They're also high in lycopene – important for protecting against cancer, especially prostate cancer.

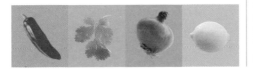

SERVES 4

PREPARATION + COOKING
10 + 12 minutes + chilling

STORAGE
Marinate the beef in advance
and keep in the fridge overnight.

SERVE THIS WITH…
leafy green salad
Fruity Quinoa Salad
  (see page 62)
Baked Pear & Spice Puddings
  (see page 129)

HEALTH BENEFITS
Walnuts are packed with
essential omega-3 and
omega-6 fatty acids, as well
as monounsaturates, which
are important for a healthy
cardiovascular system. They
lower LDL (or 'bad') cholesterol
and make the blood less likely
to clot. They also contain ellagic
acid, which has anti-cancer
properties, as well as B vitamins
for energy production.

pan-fried beef with raspberry dressing

Lean beef is an excellent source of iron and zinc, important for a healthy immune system.

1 tbsp raspberry vinegar
2 tsp crushed black
  peppercorns
900g/2lb sirloin steak
55g/2oz/¹/₃ cup walnut pieces,
  toasted

Raspberry Dressing:
3 tbsp raspberry vinegar
3 tbsp walnut oil
3 tbsp extra virgin olive oil
1 red onion, finely chopped

1 Put the raspberry vinegar and peppercorns in a large shallow dish, add the steak and turn to coat. Leave to marinate for 15 minutes.
2 Put all the dressing ingredients in a bowl, whisk well and set aside.
3 Heat a frying pan over a high heat until hot. Add the steak and sear it for 1–2 minutes on each side. Reduce the heat and cook for a further 3–4 minutes on each side until the meat is cooked but still tender. Remove it from the pan and leave to rest for 5 minutes.
4 Slice the steak thinly and arrange on four serving plates. Sprinkle with the walnut pieces, spoon the dressing over the top and serve immediately.

steak with red wine sauce

This delicious red wine sauce is full of flavour without containing any salt.

4 sirloin steaks, about 200g/ 7oz each
1 tbsp olive oil
2 shallots, chopped

80ml/2½fl oz/⅓ cup red wine
1 tbsp red wine vinegar
1 tbsp butter
freshly ground black pepper

1 Season the steaks with black pepper. Heat the oil in a frying pan, add the shallots and cook over a medium heat for 1 minute. Add the steaks and cook for 4–5 minutes on each side until cooked but still tender. Transfer the steaks to a large plate; leave to rest while you make the sauce.
2 Add the wine, vinegar and butter to the pan. When the butter has melted, let the sauce simmer over a low heat for 1–2 minutes until thickened slightly.
3 Slice the steaks and arrange them on four serving plates. Spoon the sauce over the top and serve.

SERVES 4

PREPARATION + COOKING
5 + 15 minutes

STORAGE
Best eaten immediately. Leftover steak will keep in the fridge for up to 2 days and can be served cold in salads or sandwiches.

SERVE THIS WITH...
Lemon-Paprika New Potatoes (see page 72)
steamed green vegetables
Chocolate & Orange Soufflés (see page 133)

HEALTH BENEFITS
When drunk in moderation, red wine does have some health benefits. It contains the antioxidant resveratrol, which slows down the ageing of the DNA in the body's cells. It helps control cholesterol levels and is thought to protect against heart disease and cancer.

Ⓥ ⊘

HEALTH BENEFITS
Tofu is rich in phyto-
oestrogens, hormone-like
chemicals that may help reduce
the risk of hormone-related
cancers and symptoms of
the menopause. It is also a
good source of calcium and
magnesium, important for
healthy bones and teeth.

*sweet potato & coconut curry

Tofu, or soya bean curd, is a complete
protein, which means that it contains all the
essential dietary amino acids. Mild-tasting
on its own, tofu takes on the
flavours it is cooked with
– so there's no need
to add salt.

1 garlic clove, crushed
2cm/¾in piece root ginger, peeled and grated
1 small onion, chopped
1 red chilli, deseeded and chopped
1 tbsp lime juice
1 tbsp olive oil
250g/9oz firm tofu, cut into cubes
2 tsp turmeric
1 sweet potato, peeled and cut into cubes
1 red pepper, deseeded and cut into chunks
150g/5½oz green beans, cut in half crossways
400ml/14fl oz/1⅔ cups coconut milk
1 handful coriander leaves

SERVES 4

PREPARATION + COOKING
15 + 30 minutes

STORAGE
Leftovers will keep in the fridge for up to 2 days.

SERVE THIS WITH...
Spiced Flatbreads (see page 82)
boiled rice
Spice-poached Pears (see page 135)

1 Put the garlic, ginger, onion, chilli and lime juice in a food processor and blend until the mixture forms a paste.
2 Heat the oil in a frying pan. Add the tofu and fry over a medium heat, turning occasionally, for 6–7 minutes until crisp and golden. Remove from the pan with a slotted spoon and drain on kitchen paper.
3 Add the spice paste and turmeric to the oil in the pan and cook for 1–2 minutes until the mixture bubbles gently. Add the sweet potato, pepper, beans and coconut milk. Bring to the boil, then reduce the heat and simmer for 20 minutes or until the potato is tender. Stir in the tofu, sprinkle with the coriander leaves and serve.

High-quality proteins help fill you up, stabilize blood sugar levels and keep hunger pangs at bay.

Ⓥ ✿ ⌘

sun-dried tomato, red pepper & barley risotto

Adding barley to a risotto greatly increases the protein content and gives it a nutty flavour, so you don't miss the salt.

SERVES 4

PREPARATION + COOKING
15 minutes + 1 hour + soaking

STORAGE
Make in advance and keep in the fridge overnight. Reheat in the oven.

SERVE THIS WITH…
mixed salad
Cherry & Ricotta Tarts
 (see page 132)

HEALTH BENEFITS
Barley provides plenty of insoluble and soluble fibre, selenium and copper, as well as other minerals important for health. A rich source of beta-glucan, a fibre-type complex sugar, it can help lower cholesterol levels and support the immune system.

175g/6oz/heaped ¾ cup pearl
 barley, soaked overnight
1 tbsp olive oil
1 onion, chopped
2 garlic cloves, crushed
175g/6oz/heaped ¾ cup
 arborio rice
5 sun-dried tomatoes in oil,
 drained and chopped

1 recipe quantity Roasted
 Peppers (see page 19)
4 tomatoes, peeled and
 chopped
600ml/21fl oz/2½ cups Home-
 made Vegetable Stock
 (see page 18)
2 tbsp chopped parsley
4 tbsp freshly grated Parmesan
 cheese or low-salt cheese

1 Bring a large pan of water to the boil, add the barley, cover and cook, simmering, for 35 minutes. Drain well.
2 Heat the oil in a pan, add the onion and garlic and fry gently for 2–3 minutes until soft. Add the barley and all the remaining ingredients, except the parsley and cheese.
3 Bring to the boil, then reduce the heat and simmer gently for 20 minutes, stirring occasionally, until the rice is tender. Sprinkle the parsley and cheese over the top and serve immediately.

(V) (E)

falafels with tahini sauce

This excellent protein-rich meal is a healthy vegetarian alternative to burgers.

400g/14oz canned chickpeas,
   no added salt or sugar,
   drained and rinsed
1 onion, chopped
1 garlic clove, crushed
1 tsp cumin seeds
1 tsp coriander seeds
2 tbsp chopped parsley

2 tbsp rice flour, plus extra
   for dusting
1 tbsp lemon juice
1 tbsp olive oil, for frying

Tahini Sauce:
juice of ½ lemon
2 tbsp tahini
2 tsp tamari

1 To make the sauce, put the lemon juice, tahini, tamari and 3 tbsp water in a bowl and mix well.
2 To make the falafels, put the chickpeas, onion, garlic, seeds, parsley, rice flour and lemon juice in a food processor. Pulse briefly until the mixture comes together.
3 Shape the mixture into 8 small patties. Dust them lightly with the rice flour.
4 Heat the olive oil in a frying pan, add the falafels, working in batches if necessary, and fry for 2–3 minutes on each side until golden brown. Serve the falafels warm with the tahini sauce for dipping.

SERVES 4

PREPARATION + COOKING
15 + 15 minutes

STORAGE
Make in advance and keep the uncooked patties in the fridge for up to 2 days or freeze for up to 1 month. The cooked patties will keep in the fridge for up to 4 days. The sauce will keep in the fridge for up to 1 week.

SERVE THIS WITH...
wholemeal pitta bread or Spiced Flatbreads (see page 82)
mixed salad
Spice-poached Pears
  (see page 135)

HEALTH BENEFITS
Chickpeas, lentils, mung beans and aduki beans are full of phyto-oestrogens called isoflavones, which help reduce menopausal symptoms such as hot flushes and night sweats. Tahini is a great source of calcium and omega-6 fats.

Ⓥ ✿

stuffed aubergines

This fabulous stuffed-vegetable dish is easy to prepare ahead of time – perfect for busy days.

SERVES 4

PREPARATION + COOKING
15 + 40 minutes

STORAGE
Make in advance and keep in the fridge for up to 3 days.

SERVE THIS WITH...
Mint & Yogurt Dressing
  (see page 114)
Summer Leaves with Mango
  Vinaigrette (see page 66)
Apple Crunch Cake (see page 85)

HEALTH BENEFITS
Pine nuts are an excellent source of protein and contain polyunsaturated fats that can help maintain low cholesterol levels. They are also rich in antioxidants, particularly vitamin E and zinc, important for healthy skin, heart and immune system.

2 aubergines, halved
  lengthways
1 tbsp olive oil
55g/2oz/¼ cup quinoa
150ml/5fl oz/⅔ cup Home-
  made Vegetable Stock
  (see page 18)

½ tsp ground cumin
6 dried apricots, chopped
3 sun-dried tomatoes in olive
  oil, drained and chopped
1 tomato, chopped
1 tbsp chopped mint
2 tbsp pine nuts

1 Preheat the oven to 200°C/400°F/Gas 6. Put the aubergines on a baking sheet, cut side-up. Brush with the oil, then bake for 20–30 minutes until the flesh is lightly golden and tender.
2 Meanwhile, put the quinoa, stock and cumin in a pan. Bring to the boil, then reduce the heat and simmer gently for 15–20 minutes until cooked.
3 Scoop out the aubergine flesh, leaving the skin intact. Chop the flesh and stir it into the quinoa with the apricots, tomatoes, mint and pine nuts. Spoon the mixture into the aubergine shells. Put them back on the baking sheet and bake for a further 10 minutes. Serve warm.

V ⊘ ⊳

roasted vegetables & dukkah

Dukkah, an Egyptian seasoning made with heart-healthy toasted nuts, seeds and spices, is a great substitute for table salt.

1 red onion, quartered
2 courgettes, thickly sliced
1 small aubergine, cut into
   chunks
1 red pepper, deseeded and cut
   into chunks
2 garlic cloves, crushed
4 plum tomatoes, quartered
olive oil, for drizzling

Dukkah:
4 tsp sesame seeds
1 tsp cumin seeds
1 tsp coriander seeds
1 tsp black mustard seeds
55g/2oz/½ cup unsalted
   pistachio nuts

SERVES 4

PREPARATION + COOKING
15 + 30 minutes

STORAGE
Make the dukkah in advance and store in an airtight container for up to 3 days.

SERVE THIS WITH...
Lemon-Paprika New Potatoes
  (see page 72)
Cranberry & Date Balls
  (see page 91)

HEALTH BENEFITS
Pistachio nuts are rich in beneficial minerals, including calcium and magnesium for healthy bones. Together with the sesame seeds, they provide plenty of protein, essential fats, B vitamins and vitamin E, important for heart health, brain function and healthy nerve cells.

1 Preheat the oven to 200°C/400°F/Gas 6. Put all the vegetables in a roasting tin, drizzle with olive oil and roast for 30 minutes until tender.
2 To make the dukkah, put all the seeds and nuts in a frying pan and toast lightly, stirring frequently, for 1–2 minutes until the seeds start to pop. Transfer to a plate and leave to cool for 2–3 minutes, then tip into a food processor and pulse briefly until finely ground.
3 Sprinkle the dukkah over the vegetables and serve.

SERVES 4

PREPARATION + COOKING
10 + 35 minutes

STORAGE
Make in advance and keep in the fridge for up to 2 days or freeze for up to 1 month.

SERVE THIS WITH...
couscous or quinoa
Spiced Flatbreads (see page 82)
Pomegranate-Orange Sorbet
 (see page 136)

HEALTH BENEFITS
Almonds are particularly high in vitamin E and zinc, which are important for skin health and can help prevent eczema, psoriasis and dermatitis. Almonds also contain plenty of calcium, as well as monounsaturated fats and plant sterols, which can help reduce the risk of heart disease and lower cholesterol.

vegetable tagine with dates & almonds

The vegetables, dates and almonds in this Moroccan stew are full of healthy antioxidants.

1 tbsp olive oil
1 onion, chopped
3 garlic cloves, crushed
1 tbsp garam masala
1 tsp ground cinnamon
juice of ½ lemon
1 aubergine, cut into chunks
1 sweet potato, peeled and
 chopped

400g/14oz canned chopped
 tomatoes, no added salt
400g/14oz canned chickpeas,
 no added salt or sugar,
 drained and rinsed
115g/4oz/²⁄₃ cup dried pitted
 dates, halved lengthways
55g/2oz/¹⁄₃ cup blanched
 almonds, toasted

1 Heat the oil in a large casserole. Add the onion, garlic, garam masala and cinnamon and fry over a medium heat for 2–3 minutes, stirring occasionally, until soft.
2 Add all the remaining ingredients and stir well. Bring to the boil, then reduce the heat and simmer, covered, for 30 minutes until the vegetables are tender. Serve warm.

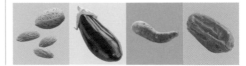

(V) (○)

lentil kedgeree & quail eggs

Brown basmati rice has a nutty flavour and keeps you feeling fuller for longer. If you can't find quail eggs, use two hen eggs, quartered.

1 tbsp olive oil
1 onion, chopped
2 garlic cloves, crushed
½ tsp turmeric
10 cardamom pods, crushed
1 tsp curry powder
300g/10½oz/1½ cups brown
    basmati rice

115g/4oz/½ cup split red lentils
2 handfuls baby spinach leaves
8 quail eggs, hard-boiled,
    shelled and halved
3 tbsp chopped coriander
    leaves

1 Heat the oil in a pan. Add the onion, garlic and spices and cook over a medium heat for 2–3 minutes until soft.
2 Stir in the rice, lentils and 750ml/26fl oz/3 cups water and bring to the boil, then reduce the heat and simmer, covered, for 20 minutes until the rice is cooked. Stir in the spinach. Serve immediately, topped with the eggs and coriander.

SERVES 4

PREPARATION + COOKING
10 + 25 minutes

STORAGE
Leftovers will keep in the fridge for up to 2 days.

SERVE THIS WITH...
Chilli & Sesame Broccoli
  (see page 70)
Pomegranate-Orange Sorbet
  (see page 136)

HEALTH BENEFITS
Lentils are packed full of heart-protecting nutrients, including B vitamins, folate, selenium, magnesium and potassium. Rich in iron and slow-releasing carbohydrates, they are great for boosting energy levels too. Combined with the rice and quail eggs, the lentils provide plenty of protein.

DESSERTS

Many processed and shop-bought desserts contain startlingly high amounts of added salt. But that doesn't mean you have to avoid all your favourite treats. The home-made delicacies featured in this chapter all offer truly satisfying indulgence without compromising on taste. From comforting Chocolate & Orange Soufflés to refreshing Tropical Fruit Skewers, there's something for everyone. The fruit-based desserts here are by far the best option if you want to cut down on the amount of salt you eat – they're naturally high in potassium to help rid the body of excess sodium, reduce water retention and lower high blood pressure. Best of all – they're delicious. Whatever you're in the mood for, you won't be disappointed.

Ⓥ ⊘ ⬡

rosewater rice pudding with strawberries

Using brown rice in this pudding provides more soluble fibre to keep you energized.

SERVES 4

PREPARATION + COOKING
10 + 40 minutes

STORAGE
Make in advance and keep in the fridge for up to 2 days.

SERVE THIS WITH...
Chicken Tikka (see page 106)
Summer Leaves with Mango Vinaigrette (see page 66)
Spiced Flatbreads (see page 82)

HEALTH BENEFITS
Strawberries contain plenty of vitamin C to help strengthen blood vessels and support the immune system, plus ellagic acid to protect body cells from free-radical damage. A great cleansing food, they are particularly useful for keeping the skin looking radiant and healthy.

125g/4½oz/²/₃ cup brown
   basmati rice or pudding rice
900ml/32fl oz/3¾ cups milk
grated zest of 1 lemon
½ tsp saffron strands
1 cinnamon stick
4 tbsp fructose
2 tbsp rosewater
8 strawberries, hulled
   and sliced

1 Put the rice in a saucepan and cover with plenty of water. Bring to the boil, then reduce the heat and simmer gently for 15 minutes until the rice begins to soften.
2 Drain well and return the rice to the pan. Add the milk, lemon zest, spices and fructose. Bring to the boil, then reduce the heat and simmer, covered, for 20–25 minutes, stirring occasionally, until the rice is tender.
3 Stir in the rosewater. Pour the rice pudding into bowls and scatter with the strawberries. Serve hot or cold.

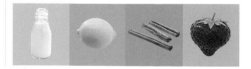

Ⓥ Ⓞ Ⓒ Ⓔ ◐ Ⓜ

baked pear & spice puddings

This delicious pudding uses dried pears, which are rich in heart healthy potassium.

150g/5½oz/heaped 1 cup dried
   pears, finely chopped
250ml/9fl oz/1 cup apple juice
1 piece stem ginger, chopped
1 tsp mixed spice
125g/4½oz/1 cup self-raising
   flour

½ tsp bicarbonate of soda
2 eggs, beaten
6 tbsp olive oil, plus extra
   for greasing
6 tbsp milk
natural yogurt or low-fat crème
   fraîche, to serve

SERVES 4 OR 6

PREPARATION + COOKING
15 + 30 minutes

STORAGE
Best eaten immediately.

SERVE THIS WITH...
Chermoula-spiced Chicken
  (see page 104)
mixed salad
Lemon-Paprika New Potatoes
  (see page 72)

1 Preheat the oven to 190°C/375°F/Gas 5. Grease and line four or six individual pudding or dariole moulds and put them on a baking sheet.
2 Put the pears, apple juice, ginger and mixed spice in a saucepan. Bring to the boil, then reduce the heat and simmer for 1–2 minutes until the juice becomes syrupy and the pears soften. Set aside and leave to cool.
3 Put the flour and bicarbonate of soda in a bowl, then stir in the eggs, oil, milk and cooled pear mixture to make a stiff batter. Spoon the batter into the moulds, cover with foil and bake for 20–25 minutes or until risen and golden. Serve with yogurt or low-fat crème fraîche.

HEALTH BENEFITS
Pears are a useful source of vitamin C, potassium and fibre, all important for a healthy heart. They also contain hydroxycinnamic acid, a powerful antioxidant that helps combat free radical damage associated with ageing.

Ⓥ ◐ Ø Ø ⊜ ⑦

HEALTH BENEFITS
Ricotta cheese is an excellent
source of calcium and is much
lower in saturated fat and salt
than many other cheeses.

*lemon-berry cheesecake

This delicious cheesecake uses nutritious
oats and almonds for a low-salt base and
features a light, luscious lemon filling.
Lemons are a great source of bioflavonoids,
such as rutin and quercetin, which work
together with vitamin C to strengthen
blood vessels, helping to prevent
varicose veins and enhance
circulation around the body.

125g/4½oz plain reduced-salt oat cakes, no added sugar
3 tbsp ground almonds
55g/2oz butter, melted, plus extra for greasing
1 tsp ground cinnamon

Filling:
2 eggs, beaten
4 tbsp fructose
450g/1lb ricotta cheese
3 tbsp natural yogurt
3 tbsp cornflour
juice and grated zest of 2 lemons
250g/9oz jar pure fruit blueberry preserve, no added sugar

SERVES 6–8

PREPARATION + COOKING
15 + 50 minutes

STORAGE
Make in advance and keep in the fridge for up to 4 days.

SERVE THIS WITH...
Chicken & Artichoke Salad
(see page 59)
Sun-dried Tomato Bread
(see page 80)

1 Preheat the oven to 170°C/325°F/Gas 3. In a food processor, blend the oat cakes until fine crumbs form. Mix in the almonds, butter and cinnamon. Lightly grease a 20cm/8in springform cake tin, press the mixture firmly into the base and bake for 15 minutes until light brown.
2 Put all the filling ingredients, except the preserve, in a blender. Process until smooth, pour over the crumb base and bake for 30–35 minutes. Leave to cool in the tin.
3 Put the preserve in a pan and heat it over a low heat for 1–2 minutes until it softens slightly. Spread it over the cheesecake and serve.

Use pure fruit spreads rather than jam as toppings for tarts and cakes to avoid unnecessary added sugars.

094

Ⓥ ⚫ ⬤ ◉

cherry & ricotta tarts

These easy tarts also make an ideal breakfast treat. Use canned cherries (in natural juice) if fresh ones are out of season.

SERVES 4

PREPARATION + COOKING
10 + 30 minutes

STORAGE
Make in advance and keep in the fridge for up to 3 days.

SERVE THIS WITH...
Lemon Chicken & Asparagus Linguine (see page 65)
mixed salad

HEALTH BENEFITS
The cherry's deep red colour comes from the powerful antioxidant compounds it contains. These support the immune system and protect against heart disease and cancer. They work together with vitamin C to help strengthen collagen, which is needed for healthy skin and blood vessels.

28 cherries, pitted
250g/9oz/1¼ cups ricotta cheese
2 egg yolks

3 tbsp ground almonds
3 tbsp Morello cherry pure fruit spread, no added sugar
olive oil, for greasing

1 Preheat the oven to 180°C/350°F/Gas 4. Lightly grease four individual 10cm/4in tart tins and put them on a baking sheet.
2 Cut 12 of the cherries in half and chop the rest.
3 Put the ricotta, egg yolks, almonds and fruit spread in a blender and process until smooth. Stir in the chopped cherries and pour the mixture into the tart tins. Arrange the cherry halves on the top.
4 Bake for 25–30 minutes until set. Remove from the oven and leave to cool before serving.

Ⓥ Ⓞ ⨂ Ⓝ

chocolate & orange soufflés

This light, yet decadent, treat is full of anti-oxidants. It is hard to believe that something so delicious can actually be good for you.

100g/3½oz dark chocolate, at least 70 per cent cocoa solids, chopped
juice and grated zest of 2 oranges

60g/2¼oz/⅔ cup ground almonds
4 eggs, separated
olive oil, for greasing

1 Preheat the oven to 200°C/400°F/Gas 6. Lightly grease six ramekins.

2 Put the chocolate in a heatproof bowl set over a pan of gently simmering water, making sure the bottom of the bowl does not touch the water. Stir until melted, then leave to cool slightly.

3 Stir the orange juice and zest, ground almonds and egg yolks into the melted chocolate. In a separate bowl, beat the egg whites with a hand-held electric beater until stiff. Gently fold the egg whites into the chocolate mixture, then spoon it into the ramekins, put the ramekins on a baking sheet and bake for 10–15 minutes until golden and risen. Serve immediately.

SERVES 6

PREPARATION + COOKING
15 + 20 minutes

STORAGE
Best eaten immediately. The soufflé mixture can be frozen, uncooked, in the ramekins. Bake from frozen for 20–35 minutes.

SERVE THIS WITH...
Pesto-crusted Chicken (see page 105)
Mint & Lemon Courgettes (see page 69)
fresh fruit

HEALTH BENEFITS
Chocolate, particularly dark chocolate with a high percentage of cocoa solids, contains antioxidants called phenols, the same chemicals that are found in red wine, which can help protect against heart disease. It also contains phenylethylamine, which creates the feel-good factor in the brain.

960

Ⓥ ⓐ ⓐ ⓐ ⓐ ⓐ

summer berry crisp

SERVES 6

PREPARATION + COOKING
10 + 30 minutes

STORAGE
Prepare the crumble mixture in advance and store in the fridge for up to 4 days. You can make and chill the dish several hours in advance, and then bake just before serving.

SERVE THIS WITH...
Crab & Fennel Salad
  (see page 58)
Sun-dried Tomato Bread
  (see page 80)

HEALTH BENEFITS
Berries, particularly blueberries, are at the top of the list when it comes to antioxidant activity. Especially good for the eyes, they help night vision and protect against macular degeneration and cataracts.

This delicious summery dessert is bursting with antioxidants from the wonderful array of fresh berries. Topped with a super-nutritious, high-fibre crumble mixture, it will boost digestion and keep your energy levels soaring.

55g/2oz/heaped ½ cup
  rolled oats
6 tbsp wheat germ
30g/1oz/¼ cup chopped
  almonds

2 tbsp olive oil
4 tbsp sesame seeds
4 tbsp hulled hemp seeds
2 tbsp honey
650g/1lb 7oz/4½ cups mixed
  fresh or frozen berries

1 Preheat the oven to 200°C/400°F/Gas 6. Put the oats, wheat germ, almonds, oil, seeds and honey in a bowl and mix well.

2 Put the berries in a large baking dish. Sprinkle the crumble mixture over the top and press down lightly.

3 Bake for 25–30 minutes until golden and bubbling. Serve hot.

(V) (⊗)

spice-poached pears

Poaching fruit is a wonderful way of enhancing its natural flavour and sweetness. This dessert uses red grape juice, which, like red wine, contains health-promoting antioxidants.

500ml/17fl oz/2 cups red
   grape juice
1 tbsp honey

4 star anise
4 Conference pears, peeled,
   with stalks intact

1 Put the grape juice, honey and star anise in a saucepan and bring the mixture to the boil. Reduce the heat and simmer gently for 10 minutes until slightly thickened.
2 Add the pears and cook over a low heat for about 15 minutes until tender. Transfer the pears to a serving dish. Strain the poaching liquid into a bowl, then spoon it over the pears. Serve hot or cold.

SERVES 4

PREPARATION + COOKING
5 + 25 minutes

STORAGE
Make in advance and keep
in the fridge for up to 2 days.

SERVE THIS WITH...
Moroccan Burgers
  (see page 115)
mixed salad

HEALTH BENEFITS
Like red wine, red grape juice contains an antioxidant called resveratrol, which helps protect the body from the effects of ageing. It is packed with anthocyanins, which help strengthen capillaries and improve circulation and heart health. Red grapes contain higher levels of anthocyanins than white ones.

Ⓥ ◈

pomegranate-orange sorbet

HEALTH BENEFITS
Compared to other juices and teas, pomegranate juice contains one of the highest levels of antioxidants, including polyphenols, tannins and anthocyanins – important for supporting the immune system and protecting the heart.

This beautiful rosy-pink sorbet is crammed full of disease-fighting antioxidants – particularly polyphenols, which are important for heart health, protecting the body against cancers and delaying the effects of ageing. The sweet oranges and pomegranate juice in this sorbet contain plenty of potassium, which is important for regulating salt levels in the body. Serve this in elegant wine glasses for a perfect summer dessert.

400ml/14fl oz/scant 1²/₃ cups pure pomegranate juice, without sugar or sweeteners
200ml/7fl oz/¾ cup freshly squeezed orange juice

finely grated zest of 2 oranges, plus extra for sprinkling
5 tbsp honey
1 pomegranate, halved
4–6 mint sprigs

SERVES 4–6

PREPARATION + FREEZING
(ICE-CREAM MAKER)
5 + 30 minutes

STORAGE
Make in advance and freeze for
up to 2 months.

SERVE THIS WITH...
Roasted Quail with Pomegranate
  Molasses (see page 108)
Fruity Quinoa Salad
  (see page 62)
Amaretto Biscotti (see page 90)

1 Put the pomegranate juice, orange juice, zest and honey in a bowl and mix well.

2 Transfer the mixture to an ice-cream maker and process according to the manufacturer's instructions until frozen. Spoon the sorbet into a freezer-proof container and freeze until firm. Alternatively, pour the mixture into a shallow, freezer-proof container and freeze until ice crystals start to form. Remove from the freezer and blend in a blender to break up the ice crystals. Return to the container and freeze until firm.

3 Hold the pomegranate over a bowl and bash with a wooden spoon to release the seeds. Scoop the sorbet into glasses. Sprinkle with the pomegranate seeds, orange zest and mint sprigs and serve immediately.

Citrus fruit contains vitamin C and bioflavonoids – antioxidants that help strengthen the walls of veins and arteries.

V

SERVES 4

PREPARATION + COOKING
10 + 17 minutes

STORAGE
Make the honey and lemon
yogurt in advance and store in
the fridge for up to 4 days.

SERVE THIS WITH...
Polenta-crusted Lamb
  (see page 113)
Orange-Honey Sweet Potatoes
  (see page 71)
Mint & Lemon Courgettes
  (see page 69)

HEALTH BENEFITS
Fresh figs are super-nutritious.
In addition to plenty of fibre and
potassium, they also contain
serotonin to help us relax.
A low intake of potassium-rich
foods, especially when coupled
with excess sodium, can lead
to hypertension.

grilled figs with honey & lemon yogurt

Grilling or barbecuing is a great way to prepare
fruit and enhance its natural flavors.

8 figs
4 tbsp honey
juice and grated zest of
  1 lemon

Honey & Lemon Yogurt:
225g/8oz/1 cup Greek yogurt
1 tbsp honey
1 tbsp lemon juice
2 tsp grated lemon zest

1 Preheat the oven to 200°C/400°F/Gas 6. To make the
honey and lemon yogurt, put all the ingredients in a bowl
and mix well. Cover and chill until required.
2 Stand the figs upright and cut them into quarters by
making two vertical cuts through each one, but do not cut
through the base, so the figs stay intact. Lay eight pieces
of foil on a baking tray and put a fig in the centre of each.
3 Put the honey and lemon juice and zest in a saucepan
and simmer over a low heat for 1–2 minutes until the
mixture thickens into a syrup. Spoon it over the figs, then
gather up the foil around the figs to form eight parcels.
4 Bake for 15 minutes until the figs are soft. Divide the
figs on to four serving plates, pour over any syrup
and serve with the yogurt.

Ⓥ ◑ ✿

tropical fruit skewers

This exotic potassium-rich dessert is a fun way
to get kids to try new flavours.

2 passionfruit
5 tbsp light coconut milk
1 tsp honey
1 banana

1 large mango, peeled and
   pitted
1 papaya, peeled and deseeded
½ pineapple, cored
olive oil, for greasing

1 Soak four bamboo skewers in water for 30 minutes.
Preheat the grill to high. Scoop the passionfruit pulp
and juice into a bowl, then add the coconut milk and
honey and mix well.
2 Cut the banana, mango, papaya and pineapple into
8 chunks each. Thread the fruit, alternating varieties, on
to the soaked skewers and brush them with some of the
passionfruit cream.
3 Put the skewers on a lightly greased baking sheet
and grill for 3–4 minutes, turning occasionally, until
lightly browned. Serve immediately with the remaining
passionfruit cream spooned over the top.

SERVES 4

PREPARATION + COOKING
10 + 4 minutes

STORAGE
Make the passionfruit cream in
advance and keep in the fridge
for up to 2 days.

SERVE THIS WITH...
Vietnamese Pork Noodles
  (see page 112)
Chilli & Sesame Broccoli
  (see page 70)

HEALTH BENEFITS
Fruit is a great source of
potassium, which is useful
for controlling the balance of
water in the body. Papayas
and bananas are particularly
rich in this mineral. Potassium
is also required by the body's
cells to respond to thyroxin,
the hormone that controls our
metabolic rate.

menu plans

wheat- & gluten-free 5-day menu

Using fresh wholesome ingredients will make it easy to ditch the salt, wheat and gluten from your diet.

Day 1
Breakfast: Pineapple, Lime & Avocado
    Smoothie (see page 23)
Lunch: Chicken Rice Paper Wraps
    (see page 50)
Dinner: Chicken Tikka (see page 106)

Day 2
Breakfast: Lemon Buckwheat Blinis
    (see page 32)
Lunch: Crab & Fennel Salad (see page 58)
Dinner: Steak with Red Wine Sauce
    (see page 117)

Day 3
Breakfast: Millet Hot Cakes (see page 31)
Lunch: Pea & Lettuce Soup (see page 46)

Dinner: Vietnamese Pork Noodles
    (see page 112)

Day 4
Breakfast: Cardamom & Fruit Compote
    (see page 26) with yogurt
Lunch: Sweetcorn & Pepper Fritters
    (see page 55), using gluten-free flour
Dinner: Baked Sesame Trout (see page 102)

Day 5
Breakfast: Baked Beans (see page 36) with
    Mediterranean Tortilla (see page 37)
Lunch: Pan-fried Salmon with Tomato
    & Bean Salad (see page 56)
Dinner: Vegetable Tagine with Dates
    & Almonds (see page 124)

vegetarian 5-day menu

This menu is designed to provide all the nutrients you need when following a low-salt, vegetarian diet.

Day 1
Breakfast: Oat Muffins with Eggs & Spinach
(see page 34)
Lunch: Roasted Garlic & Tomato Soup
(see page 45)
Dinner: Stuffed Aubergines (see page 122)

Day 2
Breakfast: Vanilla & Spice Granola
(see page 27)
Lunch: Artichoke & Onion Tarts
(see page 53)
Dinner: Roasted Vegetables & Dukkah
(see page 123)

Day 3
Breakfast: Blueberry Pancakes (see page 38)

Lunch: Balsamic-roasted Beetroot
(see page 68)
Dinner: Sun-dried Tomato, Red Pepper
& Barley Risotto (see page 120)

Day 4
Breakfast: Apple, Cinnamon & Raisin
Porridge (see page 30)
Lunch: Pea & Lettuce Soup (see page 46)
Dinner: Falafels with Tahini Sauce
(see page 121)

Day 5
Breakfast: Millet Hot Cakes (see page 31)
Lunch: Avocado & Tomato Bruschetta
(see page 52)
Dinner: Sweet Potato & Coconut Curry
(see page 118)

vegan 5-day menu

This menu avoids any foods derived from animals, including meat, fish, poultry, eggs, dairy and honey. Wherever necessary, use fortified soya, rice or oat milks, yogurts and cheeses in place of dairy products, and use maple syrup or agave nectar instead of honey.

Day 1
Breakfast: Fruit & Seed Tea Bread
    (see page 84), served with nut butter
Lunch: Roasted Red Pepper Hummus
    (see page 42)
Dinner: Vegetable Tagine with Dates
    & Almonds (see page 124)

Day 2
Breakfast: Cardamom & Fruit Compote
    (see page 26)
Lunch: Roasted Garlic & Tomato Soup
    (see page 45)
Dinner: Stuffed Aubergines (see page 122)

Day 3
Breakfast: Pineapple, Lime & Avocado
    Smoothie (see page 23)

Lunch: Fruity Quinoa Salad (see page 62)
Dinner: Falafels with Tahini Sauce
    (see page 121)

Day 4
Breakfast: Vanilla & Spice Granola
    (see page 27)
Lunch: Citrus, Bean Sprout & Avocado
    Salad (see page 63)
Dinner: Roasted Vegetables & Dukkah
    (see page 123)

Day 5
Breakfast: Millet Hot Cakes (see page 31)
Lunch: Pea & Lettuce Soup (see page 46)
Dinner: Sweet Potato & Coconut Curry
    (see page 118)

nut-free 5-day menu

Allergies to nuts and seeds are becoming increasingly common and as the symptoms can be life-threatening it is essential to take every precaution to avoid contact with nuts and by-products. This menu avoids all types of nuts and seeds. When buying any product, always check the label to ensure it is nut- and seed-free.

Day 1
Breakfast: Spicy Tomato Juice
  (see page 24)
Lunch: Lemon Chicken & Asparagus
  Linguine (see page 65)
Dinner: Seared Salmon with Gremolata
  (see page 100) .

Day 2
Breakfast: Blueberry Buttermilk Pancakes
  (see page 33)
Lunch: Butternut Squash & Pear Soup
  (see page 44)
Dinner: Lamb Koftas with Mint Yogurt
  (see page 114)

Day 3
Breakfast: Apple, Cinnamon & Raisin
  Porridge (see page 30)

Lunch: Asparagus & Herb Frittata
  (see page 54)
Dinner: Seafood Stir-fry (see page 96)

Day 4
Breakfast: Cardamom & Fruit Compote
  (see page 26)
Lunch: Lime & Chilli Turkey Burrito
  (see page 49)
Dinner: Moroccan Burgers (see page 115)

Day 5
Breakfast: Baked Eggs with Harissa
  (see page 38)
Lunch: Spicy Stir-fried Prawns
  (see page 64)
Dinner: Chermoula-spiced Chicken
  (see page 104)

INDEX